Where

the

Valley Widens

Lindsey Williams

Where

the

Valley Widens

Lindsey Williams

To My Teachers,
When They Were Just Beginning

PRELUDE
The Beginning

ALLEGRO
Years 1 – 4

YEAR ONE

YEAR TWO

YEAR THREE

YEAR FOUR

LARGO
Years 5 – 7

YEAR FIVE

SCHERZO
Years 8 – 13

CON BRIO
Years 14 – 18

CODA
The End

Dear Band,

In the beginning, I thought this was a story about you. In the middle,
I feared it was about me. Now I find it is about something else
entirely. And the end? Well, as one of my teachers would say, "It's
really too soon to tell."

Since the beginning,

Mrs. Williams

Prelude

The Beginning

July 2007

I SIT IN THE WAITING ROOM of the superintendent's office. A train horn blares in the background a block away. I glance at the old analog clock on the wall. It's 10:00 AM. The board has approved me, my certification and background check are cleared, and here I am to sign the official papers.

The central office building was obviously a school once. I don't know the story behind it, but I feel rooms full of children where offices are now. The waiting room houses the desks of four secretaries, who attend to the administrators running this entire district. The desk closest to me is decorated with strings of pictures hung like Christmas lights. "Long Train Running" plays quietly from a radio on the window ledge where philodendron vines hang just like the photos. The vines meander by the sill in search of a Methuselah tree to sink their aerial roots into, and I wonder:

Is this really the right path for me?

I am looking at the smiling faces in the snapshots when the door opens, and the superintendent, Mr. O'Dell, directs me into his office. Shadowed by his imposing stature, I feel like a guilty student walking into the principal's office. I sit, back straight, on the front third of my chair, a habit from my many years of musical training.

He swivels his black office chair up to the desk between us.

"Now," he says, "I don't mean to be blunt, but we've hired you and that means a few things. It means you need to be on time every day; not parking your car at 8:20, not walking in at 8:20. It means in your classroom, ready for students at 8:20."

I nod. He considers me without pause.

"It means you need to be here every day. Sick days are for when you are sick. They are not vacation days, or shopping days, or making-a-little-extra-cash-on-the-side days."

His eyebrows lift, and I imagine other teachers playing hooky. This man has seen it all, or at least he wants me to feel that way. It's working. Part of me wants to shrink in my seat, but I straighten my posture and meet his discerning gaze with a smile.

"Oh, I want to be here," I confirm. "That's why I applied for the job."

His black eyes narrow. He leans back in his tall chair and looks down at my résumé.

"You're coming to us from The Boston Conservatory. To teach elementary school band." He looks back at me warily and puts my papers down on his desk. "Why exactly do you want to teach in the Valley?"

It's a great question.

"Well, I grew up just a few towns over, and I missed it here."

This is not enough of an answer for him.

"Don't get me wrong," I add. "The city was great. I learned a lot studying and playing there."

He still doesn't respond, and I'm wondering how I'll tell my husband I've been fired before my first day. Clearly he's not about to let me off the hook, so I take a deep breath.

"I did train to play professionally, but when I saw for myself what that would mean—all the holidays spent gigging instead of celebrating with family, the constant need for perfection—I couldn't say I wanted it anymore." I'm not sure this is helping, but the words keep coming. "Maybe what I loved about music in the first place had as much to do with the teachers who believed in me as the music itself."

He looks up from my résumé, so I continue. "Honestly, I'm not sure exactly what I'm looking for. Maybe family. Maybe community and roots. But whatever it is, the Valley seemed like the right place to find it, and teaching felt like a good start."

Mr. O'Dell works his jaw a little, like he's chewing on a taffy. Then he takes a new manila file folder from a yellow box on the other side of his desk. He adds my papers to it and places it in the filing cabinet behind him. Then he swivels back around.

"One more thing," he says. "You are going to need a box."

I don't dare break his silence. *A box?*

"It can be any box," he continues, softer and less scripted than before, "or even just a file folder, but you are going to need it for all the letters you will receive from students and parents." He leans toward me, and I can tell he's deviating from his well-oiled spiel. "You need to put every positive thing in that box. And on the day you don't feel like being a teacher anymore, open that box and read each one."

He looks right at me and pushes the papers across the desk. I sign our contract, July 7th, 2007.

Our meeting is done, and I know my assignment: Make a box and fill it.

ALLEGRO
Years 1 - 4

"Love and death are the great gifts that are given to us;
mostly, they are passed on unopened."

~Rainer Maria Rilke

YEAR ONE

"Everything's a story. You are a story—I am a story."

From: *A Little Princess*
by Frances Hodgson Burnett

Notes

A FEW WEEKS LATER, in the heat of high summer, the school is nearly deserted as I make the maiden voyage to my classroom. Most of the hall lights are off to save the pennies of our board-approved budget. My path is lit only by a few safety bulbs and the isolated afternoon rays that sneak in through the glass emergency exit doors. Still, the winged layout and yellow cinder-block walls remind me of my own elementary school, and the place feels familiar.

As I turn down another hall toward my wing, faint voices grow steadily louder, but all I understand is their plentiful laughter. I'm about to pass by when out pops a figure from the door on my left. I step back as others file out after. In the dim lighting, I can't make out their faces, but I can see they are armed with flagpoles, ready to do battle with the latest Color Guard routine. During my initial interview, the impressive high school band director mentioned that the elementary vocal music teacher also coached Color Guard. This must be her.

"Hey, there!" she says. "You must be the new kid. I'm Becky, and no, it's not short for Rebecca—long story, I'll tell ya later. Come on kids! Jack Sparrow is waiting!"

"Arrggh!" the rest of her crew replies as they launch into the *Pirates of the Caribbean* theme song, sung in hearty unison. They stalk down the hall to their rehearsal in step with each other, and as they pass me, I see their flags are branded with the skull and crossbones.

They laugh too loudly, bantering with each other down the hall. Their sense of style is as outlandish as their laughter. Some wear edgy black outfits, others sport friendship bracelets up to their elbows, and most have their hair dyed wild hues of hot pink or neon green. This colorful bunch is a perfect crew for any pirate ship. They are so happy to be with each other, protected by summer and the haven this teacher has created for them.

I continue to Room 124, ready to use my new key, but the door is ajar on my arrival. I turn the light on and survey my domain: two green boards, an old gray desk with a stained green office chair supported by a quartet of happy tennis balls, one filing cabinet of band music, a rack of metal chairs, a few black music stands, and a clean garbage can of mismatched folding ones. It is a regular classroom, not a band room, but I feel like I've just found the buried treasure the Color Guard went in search of.

On the left-side wall, below a tidy line of coat hooks, sit trombones, baritones, percussion practice pads, and a big red bass drum. Across the length of the back wall, under three big windows, sit mostly empty metal shelves and the heating unit for the room. There appears to be no way to adjust it. On the shelves, next to a stack of dog-eared lesson books, wait a hodgepodge of saxophones and trumpets in frayed brown and green retro cases.

In the closet, I unveil a squadron of humble flutes and clarinets, their own cases uniformed in identical coats of chalk dust. Near the ceiling line, atop the built-in cabinets, sit more antique cases and drums. On the biggest bass drum, "The Academy" has been painted in the school colors of red and blue. Next to the desk, in the teacher's coat closet: I find valve oil, reeds, and a small pile of solo sheet music. That's it.

My mission is to make a band out of this.

I find a yellow legal pad and pen in the desk and begin. In the first green case I discover a wooden clarinet, mummified in old sheet music that has been unceremoniously shoved in with it. A vintage reed is still stuck to the mouthpiece. I groan and pick up the clarinet's upper joint, prying the music off its keys. The paper holds its clarinet-shaped form as I drop it in the trash bin. I can see from the instrument's fraying pads and bent keys that this will take time, patience, and intelligent work.

I empty the case of more garbage from its previous owner and secure a flopping trill key with a rubber band. By the light of the window, I can clearly make out the clarinet's serial number, make, and model. I copy it all down on my legal pad: *Boosey & Hawkes*, an old but excellent instrument maker. Then I slide the emergency window open, lean out, and set the open case in the grass to let the sun bake off its musty aroma. A stately rendition of another pirate song, "The Medallion Calls," plays on an old boom box for the Color Guard rehearsal. It drifts through my window with the sound of swooshing flags.

As I continue through these catacombs, I find that nearly every instrument hails from comparable lineage and has been equally prepared for its afterlife. I am baffled as I open case after case to find each instrument strangled in sheet music and drowning in half-eaten lollipops, their wrappers, and countless broken reeds. I vow that proper instrument care and personal hygiene will be the first things I teach the next set of fourth-grade caretakers. By the end, I have multiple garbage cans and recycle bins brimming with the artifacts of elementary instrument embalming. But I also have my first inventory, recorded on the yellow legal pad with a tidy list of needed supplies and repairs.

Most of these instruments, though old and worn, were excellent once. I can tell from the inventory numbers on their cases that many are hand-me-downs from the high school. I suspect the others are donations from former band members. Nothing is new.

I will spend countless hours of my inaugural summer bringing the ghosts of these instruments back to life, if only to an echo of their former glory. I find my earliest professional satisfaction in coaxing the first five notes of the concert B-flat scale from each of these once mighty kings.

I walk toward the single filing cabinet as "The Black Pearl" blares from the old speakers and wafts in with the breeze through my open window. There I find the music library. It stands entombed in much the same way, each title flanked by the deep blue text of mimeograph copies. I have never seen these artifacts firsthand, but I've heard from my educator grandparents of the unforgettable smell of a freshly printed ditto. I know from their stories that these copies were hard earned, one hand crank at a time, a job coveted by students almost as much as running the slide projector. I lose myself in these long-lost treasures, simultaneously dreaming of concerts past and future. Although the paper is old, the music is timeless. All but a few of these pieces will be ready for duty by the end of my summer sessions.

I'm packing up for the day when I notice the nameplate on the door. It needs an update, so I go to the desk in search of a Sharpie and an index card. I find them in the shallow center drawer along with an enormous pile of letters.

Should I read them?

They seem to be notes from students and parents. Maybe the previous teacher will want them. My curiosity wins out and I open one:

Dear Teacher,

Johnny wants to quit band. He has my permission.

Signed,

Mom

There is letter after letter of the same. The desk is full of them, all from students who've learned band isn't for them. I've heard the teacher before me was a highly respected educator and musician, but I've also heard he ended his career tired. Some even say he was driven to drink by the daily frustrations of underappreciated arts education.

I try to rationalize my thoughts away. *Band's not for everyone,* I think. *Quitting is a normal part of the job, something I'll have to get used to.* But I don't want to get used to this. I don't want a single student to learn the wrong lesson with me. I pause for a moment and think of the box I have yet to fill—or even make—and I know I cannot fill mine like this.

But as I listen to the laughter of the Color Guard crew drifting through my open window, I realize it will get filled either way. The voyage is already under way, and there's work to do. I drag my arm across the desk, bringing all that remains of this story to its final resting place in the trash among the shipwreck of old reeds and discarded treasure maps of sheet music.

Then I haul in the instruments that were baking in the sun and lock the window, turn off the light and close the door. The last thing I do is replace the little name card on the door with my own: *Mrs. Williams.* I must learn to love my place on this ship. There is too much at stake if I don't.

First Day

TODAY IS OUR BEGINNING. We don't know it yet, but it is, and I'll always remember it. I've spent summer's last weeks frantically preparing—only to arrive here at our first day feeling unready for everything.

The teachers take their places, the buses pull up to the school like synchronized swimmers, and then POW! Disorder carried on a thousand little feet descends upon our manicured grounds. "Walking feet, friends!" rings across the campus. I search for the fourth- and fifth-grade students I've been hired to help, but when I see their confident steps, I know they don't need me today. They know this place better than I do, the kingfish of this elementary pond.

Then I see a pair of hesitant feet stepping toward me. I can't believe how small he is, labeled like Paddington Bear with his pre-K name tag. It reads *Julian Finch*. Our eyes lock. We are both brand new, and in this moment, we need each other. I offer him my hand and we find his teacher, Mrs. Darling. She lines him up, like a little duckling, behind a set of brown-eyed twins in matching first-day dresses. Their tags say *Violet* and *Valerie*.

Thankfully, this expert teacher knows just how to begin. She is what everyone needs, and somehow, amid a sea of kinder-nerves, she makes space for my first-year-teacher nerves too. She lets me help even though she doesn't need it, and I send her my thanks above eleven little heads with a tentative smile. She smiles back, and instantly there are a thousand things I want to ask her.

"I hope you have a good first day," she says softly. Does she know how much I need to hear it? I can't help but wonder what's in her box, but that's all we have time for.

Off they go with her for their *first* first day of school, and off I go for mine. As I walk to my band room alone, I think about Mrs. Darling's look and I know this will be hard. I feel sure she would teach it all to me if she could, but that's not how this works. I am twenty-three, and for the first time in my life, I don't have a teacher...

I am one.

Antiques & Acronyms

IT'S THE SECOND DAY OF SCHOOL, and even though I'm early, I am not the first one here. I mumble "Gumornin" and nod my head in time with Hank, our head custodian, who is already hard at work. I'm loaded down with the day's instruments and an L.L. Bean boat bag crammed with extra supplies, snacks, and handouts I made late last night. I look like I'm headed out on a weeklong trip rather than a day at work.

I pass the before-school care group playing Simon Says in the cafeteria. Their laughter trills behind me on my way to the glass-walled office. I'm on my way to ask one of my million questions of our seasoned secretary, Mrs. Ferri, who has been here longer than the building itself and is my point person for everything.

During one of my many summer instrument repair and rehab sessions, she told me the school's life story. She remembers the old elementary school and every principal that ever led it. She remembers current staff members as elementary students themselves, and legacy educators who taught here for their entire lifetimes—teachers so adored that the roads to the new school buildings are named after them.

Mrs. Ferri knows everyone, and not just because she sits at the helm of this ship in a fishbowl office for all to see, but because her family also runs the town's taxi service. She knows where our students live, and how they live. She is our invaluable matriarch and keeper of our institutional memory.

As I approach her headquarters, I can see she is already busy putting her morning coffee to good use.

"Good Morning!" I say, reluctant to be the bother I know I am. "Sorry to interrupt, but where is the faculty meeting?"

"It's in *Dibs-N-Dabs*," she replies without looking up, fingers flying over the keyboard without missing a beat.

I look around. I don't know where or what *Dibs-N-Dabs* is, and I glance at our school psychologist, Mrs. DuBois, for help. She is always right there, steering this ship with Mrs. Ferri and our principal, Mrs. Hawkins.

"Where is Dibs and Dabs?" I ask, peering down the hall for some secret meeting room I have not yet heard of. Mrs. Ferri stops typing and smiles at Mrs. DuBois. Then she taps a stack of newly printed papers sitting on the front desk.

"*Dibs-N-Dabs*," she repeats to my blank stare. "Daily Information Bulletin."

What? My mind is slowly catching up as she hands me one. I could obviously use some coffee too.

"We put everything in here and update it daily." I look down to see *Upcoming Events*, followed by *Today's Subs* and the names of all the staff members with birthdays this month. It concludes with a *Quote of the Day*. "It's like a newspaper," she adds. I must look like I've never seen a newsletter before.

"Thanks so much," I reply. Not for the last time, I feel like a novice as I head out to face my second day, *Dibs-N-Dabs* in hand. When I get to my room, I sit at my desk to take a closer look at my newly acquired guide. It's not long before it hits me.

"Oh, it's an acronym!" I laugh out loud, alone in my room. "Daily Information Bulletin: DIBS!" My laughter continues, the joy of discovery overcoming any embarrassment. It's a good thing too, because there are plenty more acronyms and embarrassments headed my way.

Every day smacks me with something else I didn't know I had to be ready for. There are safety trainings, fire drills, and emergency dismissal procedures to memorize, along with hundreds of names. I can't keep them all straight.

After a frustrating morning of technological snafus, I knock on Becky's door once her third-grade music class is over. She's at her computer, typing away. Pirate flagpoles lean against one side of her desk, which is tucked in the corner near a tank complete with a heat lamp warming a pet turtle.

"Sorry to bother you, but who should I talk to about computer login problems?" I ask. "And is that a turtle?"

"This is Thunder, our class pet, and Chris can help you. Have you met him yet?"

"No," I answer, so she takes me down the hall to his classroom in the fifth-grade wing.

"Oh, *Mr. Goras,*" I say when I see him. "We have met. I didn't know your first name was Chris." I feel sheepish, but he doesn't seem to mind.

He shows me on his desktop how to log in and connect to the printer, and I head back to my room with his instructions. They work, so I sit down at my desk to get back to my original task: creating registration materials and instrument rental forms for tomorrow's demonstration day. While the other teachers are teaching their classes, I'm preparing to recruit mine.

I find a form from the previous teacher to use as a template, but with every word I write, I am increasingly nervous they won't choose Band. My first skirmish with the persnickety copy machine only adds to my tension. I finally leave for the day with two neat stacks of papers on my desk and a stress headache pounding behind my eyes.

The next day, I haul one of every instrument to the cafeteria and set them out with my papers. Classes file in and the high school band director, fondly referred to as Mr. F by his students, stops over to see my fourth-grade instrument demo as well. He leans against the cafeteria's side wall, arms crossed, as I play one instrument after another. My words are planned, and my enthusiasm is genuine, but I feel like a fake with his enormous integrity in the room.

Mr. F has been a well-known director in our area since I was in high school. He was even my All-County director when I was in ninth grade. He plays with the local symphony, teaches at the Big University down the road, and holds influential roles in our state music educators' association, NYSSMA. *Intimidated* doesn't seem like a strong enough word for the inadequacies I feel when I'm in front of him. He says nothing, but I fear he hears every imperfection in my playing.

As the demo classes file out, many students wave to him on their way. He waves back between friendly conversations and handshakes with the other teachers while I pack up. He's like the mayor here. Everyone knows him.

I head back to my classroom alone with my instruments and leftover papers. A few minutes later, I hear a knock on my door in the musical imitation of Dave Brubeck's "Take Five." It's Mr. F. He's carrying a four-inch red binder of curriculum and schedule templates, which he drops on my desk with a thud. For a moment, I hope he's here to compliment my demonstrations, but all he says is, "Read them. Then bring me your questions."

It's a daunting task...more like an order, really. I want to gulp and reply, *Yes sir*, but I manage to produce a normal "Thank you."

"I have to teach at the University this afternoon, but we'll talk soon," he says as he leaves the band room. I shove the binder in my boat bag and head home with my newly acquired reading material. Hours later, as I'm sitting up in bed, poring over the tome, my husband Dan laughs at me.

"What?" I say. "He said 'read it,' so I am. I can't be caught asking questions that are already answered in here. Plus, I need all the help I can get."

Dan laughs again and smiles. "Whatever makes you happy," he says.

Surprisingly, reading it does make me happy. Mr. F wrote it with the middle school director, Mr. Bishop, and it is an exquisite repository of their knowledge and values. I feel like I am reading their minds as I follow their plans for each week ahead. Every lesson—grades four through twelve, for all thirteen band instruments—has been carefully charted out. I can teach right from these pages. Though detailed and dry, it is a great comfort to know the plan and imagine how I might eventually fit into it.

After the demo, the fourth graders sign up in swarms. The fifth graders, however, are reluctant, letting me know they remain devoted to the previous director and have no interest in starting over with me. Regardless of their low participation, we run out of instruments quickly, and I am forced to attempt the next level of repairs on instruments I had initially deemed unusable.

I pull a dilapidated case down from the built-in cabinets. One latch dangles by a single screw, and the top flops open, falling away from the case it should be attached to. The saxophone inside is in equally dismal condition—beyond my skills as a repair person. I'll have to send it out. But to do that I'll have to fix the case first, so I set off for the art room, hoping to find some hot glue, or anything at all to hold the case together.

School's been out for an hour already, but the art teacher is still here setting up papier-mâché stations for the next day's lesson. I introduce myself, and my predicament.

"I'm Miss Clay," she says. "And there is a hot glue gun in the corner, or some wood glue over there if you would rather. Help yourself." I walk to the back of the room, aware that she's watching me with an artist's eye.

The room is filled with scraps of yarn, recycling, and other items that—having outlived their practical uses elsewhere—are brimming with possibility here. I feel right at home, reminded of my own childhood on the school's creative problem-solving Odyssey of the Mind team. I find the wood glue near sections of balsa wood, PVC pipes, and swaths of fabric, then I set to work mending my broken case.

"What project are you preparing?" I ask, working the wood glue's reluctant nozzle open.

"Papier-mâché puppets. The students have drawn self-portraits, and their next step is to make puppets that resemble them."

"I would have loved that project," I say.

The nozzle relents, and I run the glue between the old wooden teeth of the case's corners and fit them snugly together.

Once I've set the case with some vises I found near the balsa wood, I ask, "Can I leave this here overnight? I'll get it first thing tomorrow once it has set, so it's out of your way."

"Sure thing," she replies with a smile, unbothered by the

case or my use of her hard-to-come-by supplies. "And it's not in the way."

"Even with all my repairs, we're still about ten instruments short," I tell my mom over the phone after school that day. "We need more flutes and clarinets before we can even get started."

"Well," she says, "I was thinking about going antiquing this weekend. Maybe you and Dan should tag along and see what you find."

It sounds like a nice break. I accept her invitation, and after a Saturday morning admiring coffee table inlays and etched glass lampshades, we find ourselves in front of the *Old, Odd, and Unique Shop* at the end of Antique Row. Red Radio Flyer wagons and vintage Schwinn bikes adorn the stoop, and I see various instruments hanging in the shop's bay windows. Dan opens the door. The "OPEN" sign flams against the glass and a little bell above us announces our entrance. At the sound, the shop owner at the counter looks up from behind a set of small, silver-framed glasses that have fallen down his nose.

We putter around a bit, looking at his collection of old transistor radios, rotary telephones, and cigar boxes.

"Are you looking for anything in particular?" the shop owner asks after we have circled his room of wonders.

"Actually, yes, I'm the fourth- and fifth-grade band director at Valley Elementary School," I say, not feeling like that phrase is true yet. "We're short a few instruments at school, so I'm looking for some for our beginners."

"You've come to the right place. I have quite a few I'd be happy to show you." He climbs over a container of umbrellas, canes, and billiard cues, stepping right into the bay window's display case. He is surprisingly spry for the gray dotting his hair, and he easily passes cases of flutes and clarinets over to me until we've amassed a stout pile on his worn brown carpet. Some of the instruments will need work, but I'm surprised to find that most of them will be just fine for the fourth graders.

"How much?" my mom begins. She knows talking to strangers is hard for me and I'm no good at striking a bargain. I didn't even speak in school until the end of sixth grade. Thankfully, she and my husband both love to haggle, and apparently so does the shop owner. We finally agree to take the lot for a fair price. He helps us load them into our car and then extends his hand.

"Lonnie Dega. Pleasure doing business with you."

"Lindsey Williams," I say, shaking his hand. "I have a feeling I'll be back."

At school, the music booster club reimburses me with a check and a little note: *Best of luck with the band.* I haven't had time to find a box, so I grab an empty manila folder. I slide these first words of encouragement into it and place it in my bottom right-hand desk drawer. Then I add the instruments to our inventory and place them in the hands of students who were stranded on the waitlist. Miraculously, we get something for everyone who signed up. Now it's time to teach. Or so I think.

Even though I spend my evenings reading curriculum and writing plans, I still lack the experience and perspective needed to respond to unexpected obstacles. Nothing I have studied prepares me for the way young people see their world or the incessant inquiries of the nine-year-old mind.

"Okay," I say to a small group of beginner trumpet players who have come out of class for their first lesson. "Let's start by keeping a steady beat."

They successfully tap their feet in time with mine, but when I play rhythmic patterns for them to echo on their instruments, their feet abandon the steady pulse and follow our tones. I stop.

"Oops, you are tapping the rhythm, not the beat," I say. "Let's try again."

We do, but the same fate befalls us.

"What *is* a beat?" one student asks. The others look at me expectantly. It is so simple, I find it impossible to explain. The binder didn't mention what to do if they couldn't keep a beat. It just assumed they could, and so I did too.

"Um," I falter, working hard for my words. "It's like...that thing you dance to. Ya know, that *pulse* that never changes. Like the way your heart pounds always the same way." They just look at me, still confused. "Here, let's clap the beat to a song we already know." We do, and I barely survive the moment, only to meet countless others like it each day.

I try to tap into my conservatory teaching techniques, but I can't seem to get this ship out of the harbor. More than one clarinetist mistakes their cork grease for ChapStick and applies it before I can advise otherwise. Saxophonists lose everything from mouthpieces to neck straps in their own bells, delaying the start of their lessons until I am on the lookout for this. One trumpet player even dumps an entire bottle of valve oil into his trumpet while I am helping the others with hand position, making a slip-n-slide and a liability out of our tile floors. In the excitement of starting, numerous flutists open their cases upside down, spilling the sections of their flutes over my recently oiled floors. Hours of summer repairs are undone in an instant, and I return home each day needing more naps than the pre-kindergarteners. I knew being a teacher would be hard, and I thought I was ready—but I'm not. I am barely prepared for the teaching itself, and I'm finding out that is just a tiny part of what teachers do.

Our First Concert

THE CHAOS ONLY INCREASES with Halloween's sugar levels and Thanksgiving's five-feathered turkey handprint décor, but this is part of why I wanted to return to public school, this celebration of every season. I am comforted by each hand-snipped snowflake and schoolwide assembly, snuggled in its wintry curriculum. Classes come together over cotton ball snowmen and candy-cane crafts that taste as sweet as a snow day on our lips. This school is a more beautifully balanced ecosystem than any biologist has yet observed. Fragile, perhaps. But resilient in its ancient rhythms.

For weeks I've watched these rhythms replay my own fond flashbacks of PE parachute days, flying superman on the swings, and reading buddies, which was the only time I ever spoke in school. It feels safe, like an incubator I need as much as the students do.

But today, even with all these well-rooted customs, I am nervous.

After a fall of small-group lessons and a handful of full-band rehearsals, we have arrived at our first concert, and my morning lessons are cancelled so I can set up for the assembly.

I thought I would be excited for the impending performance, but as I trudge down the hall between my band room and the gymnasium—our big red bass drum balanced on my hip—my mind starts to race: *So many things could go wrong. What am I forgetting? I am not ready for this.* I'm near the open door of Mr. Goras's classroom when I pause to shift the drum to my other hip.

"Okay, let's get up and move a little before our next mini-lesson," he says. They quickly assemble around their campfire carpet. He cues up the music and they launch into an enthusiastic rendition of "Fifty Nifty United States," which I know from my youth. My nerves lift a little.

Further down the hall, I pass a probably-first-grader with light-up sneakers humming "The Ants Go Marching" to herself as she takes a worn wooden bathroom pass on one of its numerous daily walks. I hum her tune and sections of "Fifty-Nifty" as I set up chairs and stands and lunches begin. Soon I cannot hear myself over the shenanigans coming from the faculty room and the laughter from the cafeteria next to it, and moving helps distract me from wondering once again if I have made the right choice, trying to be a teacher. It was within walls just like these that I first discovered I was a musician, with a teacher who saw more in me than I saw in myself. *Do I have what it takes to be this for my students?*

After lunch, I'm running the last milk crate of sheet music to the gym when I pass Mrs. Burnwood's first-grade classroom. She is settled in her read-aloud rocking chair, and I hear the words of E.B. White's *Charlotte's Web*. It sounds as if she's reading it as much for herself—and secretly for me—as for her pupils, and it's the best sort of comfort I could receive today.

Each year, these rituals mean more. Students come to school with anticipation, knowing this is their year to hatch monarchs, take the historic walking trip around town, conquer the Great Escape Obstacle Course in PE, or become their favorite character in the parade of good books. This year, many have joined the band, and today is one of the days they arrive looking forward to: the first concert.

Well, technically, it's a dress rehearsal we've invited the entire school to enjoy. The din of five hundred December-infused children's voices begins to fill the gymnasium as the band and I wait to perform our Winter Concert. I am still nervous, but just as calmed by our band and chorus, wiggly in their ready positions, as I am by all the rows of children who know just how to sit, "crisscross-applesauce-spoons-in-the-bowl." The teachers lead their ducklings, making sure the ones with that extra sparkle in their eyes have a seat right next to their mother duck.

Each class files into their customary place, and I'm thankful this part happens without my help directing. The pre-K class follows Mrs. Darling and sits up front so they can see. I see the brown-eyed twin sisters and the little Finch I helped on the first day. He is taking in this scene for the first time, much as I am. It feels like everyone else has been here forever, whether they predate us by one year or thirty. They have a collective memory that spans generations, giving them an ease I truly envy.

Yet I am the only band director these pre-K's will ever know. So when I speak to my first audience ever, I think of Julian, and the twins, and not my fear. If I do my job right, they will leave today dreaming of being a fourth grader and of the day they hold their own instruments for the first time.

I open the concert with scripted words that do not yet feel like my own, the shy student in me balking at the public speaking this job requires. Then I lift my hands for the first time in concert. They are shaking. Being on display like this, as a first-year teacher, feels like entrusting my livelihood to a pack of wild ferrets. But miraculously, the band members lift their instruments and we play "Jingle Bells," just like we practiced. Even more miraculously, we end together and I turn to the audience, feeling the support of the entire school in their applause.

Mrs. Darling finds the faces of her adored alumni and sends them specific smiles, knowing their stories and how hard it is for so many of us to show our current selves on that stage. Miss Clay claps for the children as if they are her own, and I understand for the first time that in some secret way, they are. I still feel insufficient, but as we bow, I see Julian's and the twins' eyes looking up from the first row. They are bright and round and enchanted, and even though I don't know much yet, I know they are already in the band.

Jazz Band

"WE'D LIKE YOU TO START a Jazz Band," Mr. F had said in the interview, "at the elementary school."

Okay, I'd thought. *I can do this*. If they expected eight-year-olds to do it, then I—with my Music Master's and conservatory training—certainly could too.

Couldn't I?

Just to be sure, I spent the fall taking my own set of lessons at the music shop two towns over. Each Thursday, I hustled there after school to work on my ii-V-I progressions and expand my blues vocabulary with the most respected jazz pianist in town. He and his studio were seasoned with years of cigarette smoke and cheap coffee, so his students were blessed with a second-hand buzz in addition to their mixolydian scales, free of charge. I left with more than enough material and jazz aura for my fifth-grade improv endeavors. Hopefully, my lagging confidence would catch up.

Today, with our first Winter Concert complete and my own education well under way, I make my announcement: "We are going to start a Jazz Band!"

And with that simple sentence, it is real.

I pass out papers with details and set audition material just slightly harder than the music they can currently play. That's all it takes for the excitement—and practice—to ensue in earnest. Lunches and recesses percolate with the sounds of wannabe jazz cats cutting their teeth on the changes of their *Maiden Voyage* audition rep. Scales that have remained neglected are now quickly memorized. I watch as students wrestle with the two sturdy notes of "C-Jam Blues," standing sentry to their future in our prestigious elementary jazz program. The possibility of failure eggs them onward.

After two weeks, I post a blank audition signup sheet, and its lines fill rapidly with the teetering signatures of newly acquired cursive. Fifth graders scribble over the bumps of our cinder-block walls with a lonely pencil leashed to its paper with a sad bit of string and tape. (A pen, I've learned, cannot endure a single attempt at elementary wall writing.)

The next week of practice crescendos toward audition day, as brave little troupes stop by to reserve a chance to prove their readiness. I hear their giggles and hushed conversations outside my door as they encourage each other to take the leap. On the last day, I see beneath my door the shadow of one who comes alone under the never-failing cover of a trip to the bathroom. Only I see his name, added in tiny letters to the bottom of the list in the eleventh hour. Only I know just how much he has practiced. He has hidden his hope from everyone else, most of all himself.

When auditions arrive, wobbling knees and trembling fingers file in and out of the band room doors in procession. I smile, hoping to ease their fears, but on this day I might as well be the *Band Director from the Black Lagoon*. I've already written to their parents and reminded them in class: "If you are not ready for disappointment, you are not ready to audition." The words seem harsh for elementary school, but it's a lesson that only gets harder to learn. Of course, there are some tears. Some cry before they even enter the room. Others brush it off like it is nothing. The last to audition is a boy named Zach—the boy who signed up alone at the bottom of the list. He walks in, shoulders hunched, hiding his face with his hair.

"Let's start with your C Scale," I say.

Without a word he lifts his trumpet, trying to prove that all his practicing has paid off. His fingers are shaking above the valves, but he launches in and finishes the audition without a single tear.

"Thank you for playing today," I say as I see him to the door. "The list will be posted first thing tomorrow."

They've all done well, and truthfully, I need each one of them. I don't plan to make any cuts today.

After the buses leave and the halls are quiet, I sit with my back to the dimming light of my winter window. There I write each of their names in the spots they've all so bravely earned. I place them in positions that complement each other's strengths, weaknesses, and personalities. I've already enjoyed pairing students with the perfect instrument. Pairing them with each other proves to be much more difficult, but just as satisfying in the end.

I tidy up my room and post "The List" on the bulletin board outside my door. Then I walk to my car under the dark 5:00 PM January sky, nodding *Good Evening* to the second-shift custodians on my way out. For one night, the list hangs there with all its secrets in plain sight while thirty fifth graders dream of reading their names there tomorrow.

The next morning, a horde of students rush to my room. Many who didn't even audition are there, ready like town criers to spread the breaking news throughout fifth-grade classrooms and beyond. I come to the door to witness their realizations of success and pass out papers—complete with detachable permission slips—for our after-school practices.

I marvel at how easy it is. I simply typed up the pages, made the announcements, and *Voila!* I feel like I just made it all up, but to them this is our Official Jazz Band.

As the mob disperses, Zach slowly approaches the bulletin board. His shoulders slump. His long hair covers one side of his face in an effort to hide the scars from his cleft palate surgeries. The last to sign up and the last to audition, he is now the last to step up and see "The List." He methodically reads every name, not expecting to find his own.

Then he sees it. His eyes open wide, and he shakes his hair back to get a better look, hope un-hunching his shoulders for the first time. There he is, nestled in the trumpet section.

"*I made it*," Zach whispers to himself in wonder, a smile spreading across his whole being. These are the first words I hear him say, and the first time I see him smile. Neither will be the last.

He finishes reading the list and turns, still awestruck and oblivious to my presence. His permission slip still lies in my outstretched hand as I watch him walk down the hallway, shoulders and hair back, smiling all the way. I am dumbstruck by all the good that's come from a few made-up paragraphs and a pencil that still hangs on a string by my door. I know by the way he walks down the hallway that he will never walk that other way again.

I watch him till he turns the corner, and with the same sense of disbelief and wonder, I whisper it too: "I made it."

Summer Lessons

DESPITE THE DECENT PROGRESS of the Jazz Band, I fumble through the spring much as I did the fall, every day presenting me with unexpected educational fires to put out. Even after nearly a year, I still feel like a stranger here. Jobs are hard to come by, and there are no other new teachers in my building to ask, "Is it hard for you too?" On the contrary, most of my professional conversations revolve around techniques for avoiding head lice with people who are just hitting their double digits.

A group of six fourth-grade flute players and I are packing up from our last lesson of the year when one of them nervously approaches me.

"Do you give private lessons over the summer?" The words tumble from her in a swan dive of risk into the waters of adult conversation.

"Sometimes I do, Anne." My quiet-kid empathy rises with every word, and I lead her along. "Are you interested?"

"Yeah. My mom said to ask you about lessons for me and my brother Jeremiah. He'll be in fourth grade next year. He wants to play the trumpet." She rolls her eyes back at the thought of her brother.

"Okay, is she picking you up today?" I ask. "I can talk with her then."

"That's perfect!" She sighs with relief at the conversation's conclusion.

We finish cleaning and sanitizing our instruments and set them in tidy rows for summer storage. They await next year's students in a much different state than they did last July. After only a year, it's hard to pinpoint the improvements I've made, but this is progress I can see. *If I can't be good at this yet*, I tell myself, *at least I can be organized and kind*. My student seems to appreciate both as she continues packing up for dismissal.

Our pickup and drop-off times are always exploding with elementary energy, and today is no different. The accomplishment of another completed school day arrives at exactly 3:15 PM with the long-anticipated beep and the familiar voice of Mrs. Ferri: "May I have your attention for the afternoon announcements. Reminder: Please remember to wear your red, white, and blue for tomorrow's Flag Day ceremony with the Daughters of the American Revolution. Walkers and permanent-pickup riders are now dismissed. Will the following students please report to the main office for dismissal..."

Then commences the list of frequently read names that somehow never make it to the permanent-pickup list. I am grateful for this daily oration because it's how I learn to pronounce the names of many future band members. I arrive at my bus duty post near the main office, where I witness the joy of hearing one's name on this sacred list and the hidden speed-walking skills of third graders. I smile and wonder if anything *in* school will ever enthuse these students as much as leaving it does.

After reminding many would-be runners of the benefits of

walking, I seek out Anne's mom. She's in her usual spot, her pre-Ker hanging from her and every available anchor like a capuchin monkey as she waits for her older children.

"James, please," she says, prying him off her. We chat about summer lesson details and agree on a weekly time at her house. My husband Dan will teach Jeremiah trumpet while I teach Anne my primary instrument, the flute.

"Can't wait," I say. "See you the first week of July."

On our first drive to the hillside development across town, Dan and I are both excited, happy to be teaching private lessons on our primary instruments, a comfort zone for both of us.

"This should be fun," Dan says. "I've never taught a complete beginner before."

Dan is finishing his own studies at the University near our home, but he's been an excellent trumpet player since high school, where we met.

"He is a complete beginner on trumpet, but his mom said he's had piano lessons and knows how to read music a little."

"Still," says Dan, "he's not even in fourth grade yet. That's pretty young. He's going to have a great head start."

We arrive at our student's house for the first lesson, prepared with practice logs, scale sheets, and lesson books. I am guided to a spinet piano in the corner of the living room for Anne's flute lesson, while Dan is directed to a side room with Jeremiah. As the two trumpeters walk down the hall, I overhear their awkward first attempt at conversation.

"So you've taken some piano lessons before," my husband starts up.

"Oh yeah, loads of 'em. I know how to read music and that a C-sharp is basically the same as a B-flat." I smile. This one is hungry to prove himself, and we also have some work to do.

"I see, so you know about enharmonics," Dan says. "We can work on those with the trumpet too."

"Oh yeah. I'm very interested in learning the C-sharp major scale on trumpet," Jeremiah continues. "It should be pretty simple since I already know how a major scale goes: Whole, Whole, Half, Whole, Whole, Whole, Half."

"Excellent! Well, let's get started with opening the case and learning how to buzz, and we'll be learning those scales in no time."

I can barely contain my laughter, relishing this exchange between the most knowledgeable and enthusiastic almost-fourth-grader I might ever meet and my gentle husband on his first teaching assignment.

I turn to Anne, who is busy readying her music and assembling her flute. In a private lesson, I can tailor everything to her, so I take the time to set her mouthpiece slightly off-center to account for the natural curve of her lip. She tries the new setup and is instantly impressed with her resulting tone.

We are just beginning to play at the piano when I hear a little thump behind me. Peeking out from behind the sectional sofa is the curious capuchin child from pickup. He playfully retreats to escape my gaze, which I have the distinct feeling he sees as lasers.

Anne sighs. "That's my littlest brother. He's starting kindergarten this fall and wants to play the drums. His name is James."

We return to our lesson, Anne making steady progress to the equally steady soundtrack of James playing *floor is lava* and *music teacher's eyes are laser beams*. With no other students playing along, I hear her clearly, and with a few simple exercises we clear up the articulations in the solo she is working on. Anne hears the improvement too, and I finally feel in my element after a year of lessons outside my comfort zone.

I savor this, wishing I could teach private flute lessons all day, giving each student my full attention and the very best of my expertise. I enjoy the rare feeling of knowing I have done a good job. We've finished the lesson and begun packing up when James somersaults over the back of the sofa. As he vaults into a perfect landing I think, *He certainly has the energy and coordination to drive an entire band. He will be an excellent drummer.*

As Dan and I leave, their mother also mentions that James would like to learn the drums. I give her the number of our famed high school band director, Mr. F, who is a well-respected percussionist. She vows to call him as soon as gravity can hold her acrobat urchin in one place for a thirty-minute session. He peeks out from behind her leg. He's heard every word, even though I've yet to hear one from him. As we head to the car, I hear him resume his practice with the rhythmic thuds of a promising percussionist. His steady steps have told me all I need to know. He is already a musician. And I only have four years to make my percussion lessons just as strong as my flute ones, so I can be ready for him.

YEAR TWO

"Tell all the truth but tell it slant —
Success in Circuit lies
Too bright for our infirm Delight
The Truth's superb surprise"

From *Tell all the truth but tell it slant —*
by Emily Dickinson

Slant

SOMETIMES YOU NEED A SIGN. Summer is over too quickly, and—despite my preparations, my successful lessons with Anne, and my now year of experience—a pang of dread hits me whenever I think about the approaching large-group rehearsals. I'm still not sure how to help them progress together, the way I've been able to help Anne on her own. I'm still not sure if my coworkers see me as anything more than a burden, with all the things I still don't know.

In short, I'm still not sure if I'm going to be good at this.

I'm standing at the main office counter, asking the all-seeing Mrs. Ferri and Mrs. DuBois one of my zillion questions, when Miss Clay is suddenly by my side in a swirl of hippie skirts and colorful headband scarfs. She points a dry paint brush in my direction.

"Just the person I was looking for!" exclaims the Miss Frizzle of fine arts and finger paints, arms wide open with triumph.

I look behind me but see only the well-labeled rows of faculty mailboxes and a blue food drive donation bin.

"Me?" I say, turning back around and nearly bumping into

the bin.

"Of course, you! We need an Odyssey of the Mind coach and I've seen what you can do with a bottle of wood glue. You'd be perfect. Odyssey of the Mind is a team-based, creative problem-solving program," she recites like a living instruction manual.

"Oh, I don't know," I hedge, still unsure of myself. Either she doesn't hear me or she's pretending not to.

"Coaches are just that—only coaches. You can't tell the students anything. You can only ask them questions and help them find the materials they choose to solve their problem."

"I know," I reply quietly, not sure if I should add the next sentence. But I do: "I was in it as a kid."

"I thought so." She smiles with satisfaction over her waggling paintbrush, and I feel like I have known her for a thousand lifetimes. My instrument repair session in her room obviously gave me away. "There's a meeting after school Monday," she continues. "See you there."

It isn't a question.

She is gone in the same swirl that sent her to me, and now I have a date with my first ever after-school activity. Stunned, I turn back to Mrs. DuBois' and Mrs. Ferri's wry smiles. We've forgotten whatever was so important, having witnessed Miss Clay's wild magic at work. She's signed me up, and it feels like freedom as I'm swept into her creative maelstrom.

Monday arrives before Friday feels over, and Odessey of the Mind (OM©) instructions are seamlessly threaded into the afternoon announcements before anyone can say *Abracadabra*. I report to Miss Clay's room as directed—still wondering what happened to my weekend—to find a plethora of parents and snacks awaiting me. Each team has been paired with their coach by the hand of an artisan who has certainly done this before. I am swiftly herded to my fourth- and fifth-grade team, most of whom I thankfully know from Band Land. My summer students, Anne and Jeremiah, are among the seven of them.

As we get settled, I am astonished by the number of students and parents who are smiling and laughing, excited to spend even more hours at school after long days in the classroom or at work. The primary team of kindergarten, first, and second graders flock to their coach, Mr. Wall, an involved engineer dad who settles them with apparent ease. I'm impressed, still being somewhat intimidated by large groups of the littlest ones myself.

With him I see little Julian Finch, the sofa-acrobat James, and Violet and Valerie, the brown-eyed twins from Mrs. Darling's line last year. I find myself drawn to their faces, as if I can measure my own growth with theirs. Little do I know, Mr. Wall and the other parents in this room will become the familiar faces of our band fans and family for years and years to come. They will build magnificent musical sets and work sound and lights for concerts. This is just the beginning of their long-standing, devoted involvement with their children and our schools.

Miss Clay gives us everything we need: an overview, the coach's guide, a problem packet to choose from, and of course, a snack. Apple juice and animal crackers never tasted as good as they do today. They encourage us to brave what lies beyond the box, after another austere Monday of the American Education System and its national initiatives for everything but the arts. Our team chooses projects, sets a recurring meeting time, and finally disbands for the day.

On my way out, I see a lonely clothespin clipped to Miss Clay's computer, decorated with simple bands of yellow and orange marker. It's inscribed with a single word written in fine-tipped Sharpie, so faded by the sun I cannot make it out.

I sense it is meaningful, and I am left wondering about it on the entire walk to my silver Toyota Corolla.

Every Wednesday and Friday after school—October through March—as the building's heater punctually clunks off with the close of the day, the band room erupts with so much more than music. Empty paper towel rolls and recycled artifacts of all kinds are held together with rubber bands, paper clips, big ideas, and the ludicrous laughter of my Seven Stooges.

They hone a solution to their chosen "long-term" problem and write a hilarious skit to present it with, per the packet's instructions. Their lines are as outrageous as their personalities, and their flare for drama increases with every meeting. This bunch thrives most on each other and shines even brighter when solving problems in the "spontaneous" section. With no time to plan, their unconventional instincts take over in the divergent ways this program is built to encourage.

As I work closely with this small group—where I'm not allowed to be in charge—I notice myself shifting, developing more creative ways of questioning the students. As the months progress, I even try some of the techniques with my band and find that they work there too. Our team meets daily in the final weeks before the March competition, and even though I'm tired, excitement overrides my increasing exhaustion.

On the big day, we unload our creations from family minivans and haul them down long halls packed with costumed kids and their own projects. Then we find our room and wait. Containing my team's excitement is the hardest part of my job so far.

When their time to take the stage finally arrives, my group performs with a verve I haven't seen before. Their cooperation is seamless, their skit is hysterical, and their solution is so clever we all wish we'd thought of it. The judges don't give away much, but I'm pretty sure I catch a little smile from the one on the right. We watch the other teams from our school perform, and after each one there are hugs and handshakes from students and parents alike.

Then it is on to the spontaneous section of the program. The team enters, but no audience is admitted for this secret portion of the competition. I wait outside with their parents, and every few moments we pause our conversations, straining to hear anything we can from inside the room. When they emerge, the team says nothing, but their giddiness betrays the success they must have had.

We pack up and wade through the crowd to the gym for the awards ceremony. Waiting for the results is even worse than waiting for our turn to perform. The awards ceremony begins with a celebration of the non-competitive primary division. My team cheers with gusto for Mr. Wall's, but our nerves jitter more with each announcement that isn't ours.

Finally, they come to our division. Anne and Jeremiah both hold their breath, and my team huddles closer together as they wait.

"The third-place prize goes to...the Hampton School District's Fourth and Fifth Grade Team!" My entire team exhales because it's not our name and they grab each other's hands, not knowing where to put their pent-up energy.

"And second place goes to..."

My students shut their eyes, still not breathing, and I'm afraid they might pass out from lack of oxygen. "Valley Elementary School's Fourth and Fifth Grade Team!"

We all holler in celebration. Jeremiah whoops in triumph, high-fiving the boy next to him. Anne finally inhales again, bouncing on her toes excitedly and embracing the other members of our team in an epic seven-person group hug. Our second place feels like first, and my team members bound arm-in-arm to the stage to receive their trophy. As I watch them, I see how they have grown, but that doesn't feel like the most important thing this experience has given them.

OM families meet the next Saturday for a final celebratory meal at Miss Clay's abode. We laugh so hard, our sides hurt for hours, and my smile stretches into Sunday. When I return to school for the next work week and reach to start my computer, I am surprised to see a simple faded clothespin clipped to the top of my screen. I unpin it, and upon inspection decipher the single faded word I could not read in the art room.

Friendship.

Alone at my desk, I hear their laughter, and I see her smile, and I know my empty room is full of friendship. If I had a box, maybe I would put this in it. But I don't yet, so I leave the clothespin clipped to my screen, knowing it will fade even further in the morning light.

I stop in the art room after school the next day. Miss Clay is preparing stations for tomorrow's Kindergarten class on scissor safety, and she looks up at the shadows my silhouette draws across her doorway.

"I got your gift," I say.

I want to add, *Thank you for asking me to be on the team. Thank you for knowing how to do it and knowing that I could too. Thank you for making it fun. Thank you for your friendship.* But all I manage is "Thanks."

I pray my smile conveys all the things I cannot say. My best words have learned to hang hidden behind my tongue, afraid they will spook others away with their awkward rawness. Considering that I did not speak for any of my own elementary school experience, I figure I'm doing quite well.

Written words were the ones that always spoke to me. I read my favorites on repeat, like a silent mixtape of my most cherished songs. I played Emily Dickinson the most, and my favorite of hers remains: "Tell all the truth but tell it slant." Well, music and silence are my truth. *Slant* is the only native language I speak. Thankfully, Miss Clay is fluent too. I should have known.

She puts her scissors down. "That clothespin was given to me by George Thearle during my first faculty meeting. I've held onto it for a while, but I thought I would pass it on to you." At the mere mention of his name, my mind rushes to memories of our previous principal.

I met him only once, and I know first impressions aren't everything. But he certainly impressed me. Everyone in that school loved him. The bones of the school itself loved him, their adored and chosen captain. I was Mr. Thearle's last hire.

"Let me introduce you to our new principal," he said as he passed me on to her. "Principal Hawkins is starting today too. I know you will love her." So I did. I loved her because he said I would, and I trusted him. His leadership was strong, honest, and kind.

Miss Clay gestures to a simple piece of paper hanging near her desk.

"I still have this page from George." Her eyes move from it to me as she speaks the words written there by heart: "Be brave. Even when you're not, no one can tell the difference."

It's the moral of Mr. Thearle's story. One she loved so well, he left it with her. Now she guides his gift onward.

"I hang it right by my door," she says, "and read it every time I wait for a class."

I've seen the sign before, but always assumed it was for her students—not for her, my mage of wild magic.

The next day I bring in my own sign, a Kipling poem I've loved since high school, with the shortest title I can imagine: "If."

I've read it hundreds of times, and each time different lines stand out to me. Today it is the two in the first stanza about making allowance for the doubts of others.

> *"...If you can trust yourself when all men doubt you,*
> *But make allowance for their doubting too..."*

These first two years have felt like this, learning to address my mistakes without losing faith in myself. I hang the poem on the wall with a bit of Scotch tape, and it looks over me and my clothespin. I've got my own sign now—some art to encourage me through the dark until I have a box to open.

Years from now, after time and love have carried Miss Clay to far-off ceramic studios in New England's finest boarding schools, I will ask her about her sign over coffee. She'll tell me she still has it, hanging on the wall by her door. She still reads it while she waits for each class to arrive, and somewhere George Thearle smiles, knowing his words slant ever onward.

Siblings

SIBLINGS ARE EVERYWHERE at school, but you notice them most at arrival, lunch, and dismissal. As these spring mornings get warmer, I see toddlers loaded in red wagons attending the drop-offs of their bigger brothers and sisters at the elementary school. At lunch, I see the brown-eyed twins sitting side-by-side, swapping snacks and juice boxes from their matching brown paper bags. In the afternoons, I watch the high schoolers traverse our campus from the secondary school across the field, visiting past teachers before chaperoning their kid kinsmen home.

Some students' eyes light up when I assign them the same saxophone their brother shuffled home with for years. Other siblings, however, walk in opposition—studious flutists like Anne, followed by jaunty cornetists like Jeremiah. Somehow, whatever the combination, brothers and sisters often embody the lessons their siblings need most. They are the only messengers equipped with the sass and spunk needed to deliver words their kin can hear from no one else.

When the youngest aren't being herded by their siblings, they are often carried by their parents, regardless of their ability to walk. Families with many children become mainstays of our schools, their parents' faces as familiar as the teachers at open houses, year after year, for decades.

I first hear about one such family, the Finches, from Becky in the last weeks of my second school year.

"Oh, the Finchlettes!" she says during our customary hallway hustle to the "little teachers' room" after a regimented morning marathon of classes. "They are all so musical. Just wait till you get them."

"I met Julian Finch my first day here, and he was in Odyssey of the Mind," I say.

"The older two are just as endearing! Arthur played his violin at the talent show last year, and Lynn danced. All three are learning string instruments from their mom," Becky continues over the soap dispenser and a wimpy trickle of water. "Arthur will be in fourth grade next year, so I'm sure you'll meet them soon."

We wash our hands to the familiar pink scent of cherry-almond and shake them dry, ignoring the brown papery towels we know lack the ability to absorb anything. The faculty bathroom's slender door opens onto a dim little hallway that leads to our lunchroom. Our hideout is constantly brimming with fantastic tales and exasperations.

My favorite storyteller, Mrs. Marion, is just beginning her morning report as we take our usual seats by Miss Clay at the brown banquet tables. A mismatched set of plastic-back classroom chairs rings the tables' U-shaped setup. These surviving chairs have somehow withstood years of tiny toes tipping them backwards, only to be reunited with larger versions of those same feet on adults who have just as hard a time keeping "four-on-the-floor."

"In first grade today," Mrs. Marion begins, "Mrs. Burnwood opened the bathroom door to find a turd stuck in the ceiling vent." All side conversations hush at her well-placed opening. "And the last person to use it was little Teddy."

"Oh, Teddy," flits through the room, a shared sentiment on the lips of all the teachers who've had him.

"She asked him what happened, but he wouldn't say, so she sent him to Mrs. Hawkins' office," Mrs. Marion continues. "She couldn't get him to talk either, but Mrs. DuBois had the brilliant idea to go get his sister, RuthAnn. RuthAnn said he just needs a snack when he gets like that. So we made sure he washed his hands and got him some goldfish crackers. While he was eating, he finally told her, 'Sissy, *it just jumped right up there*.'"

Our boisterous laughter is so loud, I'm sure it can be heard a hallway away.

"I would have liked to see Hank's face when he got the call to perform an overhead excrement extraction," she announces over the eruption.

As a new member of this secret society, I am quiet, mostly listening to casual conversations roll through every topic. About halfway through lunch, the chatter finally lands on the frustrations that are truly occupying everyone's minds.

Mr. Goras sighs over his sandwich and the pile of math corrections he's been reviewing. "I'm just hitting a wall with Ella and fractions." He puts his lunch down, which is unusual. He is tall and skinny and always hungry. "Today she was so frustrated she gave up, and I nearly did too."

Becky chimes in. "Oh, I'll see what I can do. Ella loves singing, and I've got ways to weave in fractions without her ever knowing she's learning math in music class!" She smiles deviously over her Mountain Dew and leftover Chinese takeout.

"Incidentally," another conspirator offers, "I observed a few things about Ella's application of math concepts in science the other day..."

While Mr. Goras and the science teacher trade bits of lunch and teaching tips, my mind drifts to the oldest Finch. I'll meet him this September, and I want to pair him with the perfect instrument. I smile as a hunch develops. Of course, I will need to see how they take to each other. Or if the Finches are even interested in learning other instruments. Some students—and parents—are not.

I open my own lunchbox to a smorgasbord of my favorite foods, remembering one of my past teachers who insisted success came only to those who dedicated themselves to a single discipline. Her advice cleared my path to the Conservatory and the success I sought. I know how well it worked, but I hope I can teach my own students without this exclusion in the name of excellence. That teacher and I worked together for years, as is the custom in our music world, until she'd taught me everything she'd learned from her teacher. The connection was the closest I had to anyone except my parents.

The truth is, I am still looking for that connection with a teacher. Even through Conservatory, I was always anchored by the guidance of mentors, and now as a young teacher, I've often felt rudderless. I've finished Mr. F's big red binder, and each evening I now lose myself in the pages of *One Band That Took a Chance*—a book about a high school band director named Frank Battisti who went on to conduct bands at the highest collegiate and professional levels. He conducted at a summer band camp I attended as a high schooler and remains the most inspiring person I've ever played for. His words give direction to my now somewhat unattended professional growth, and I practice his instructions just as hard as I used to for my private lessons.

"Don't forget—" Miss Clay's voice pulls me back to the

conversation in our faculty classroom "—tomorrow's Club Fed."

"Get ready! I'm bringing my famous Buffalo Chicken Dip," says Becky.

During the week, many teachers (myself included) duck in to heat up and consume last night's leftovers on communal dishes before scooting back to our classrooms for the afternoon stretch. But on Fridays everyone comes to "Club Fed," fifth grade's infamous potluck party.

Pairs of us take turns cooking for the others. Cornflake casseroles and chicken-parm-pasta-bakes soothe our worries and appetites. As loved as Thanksgiving Dinner, Club Fed connects us over mismatched plates of each other's favorite recipes. Each of us brings something we know the others enjoy. Each of us leaves ready for the weekend and renewed for another week of worksheets and read-alouds. After all, another week means another Club Fed.

Sometimes we don't know what we were missing until it's sitting there, part of the potluck in front of us. It might not be what we're looking for, but it nourishes all the same. And here, in our only adult space, we teachers give and get what we need, becoming something much more than coworkers over Mrs. Marion's tales and chocolate chip cookies. As summer approaches, I realize I'm going to miss these raucous feasts until next fall.

Maybe I do need a mentor. I've been poring over every book hoping to find one. Maybe what I really need is several of them—something like siblings, crowded around our tiny table in mismatched chairs, trading lunches and laughter, saying all the things our past teachers couldn't tell us.

YEAR THREE

"Sometimes she stopped digging to look at the garden and try to imagine what it would be like when it was covered with thousands of lovely things in bloom"

From *The Secret Garden,*
by *Frances Hodgson Burnett*

Cases

IT'S OPEN HOUSE IN MY THIRD YEAR when I finally meet the
Finches: Mom, Dad, and the trio of Finchlettes. They flock
together down the hall to my room as Open House nears its
end and the flow of families has subsided to a trickle. The older
two, a boy and a girl, stand silently beside their mother. The
youngest, busy being six in his father's arms, has a bird's eye
view of the conversation.

"This is Arthur." Their mother gestures to the oldest. "And
Lynn." She puts her arm around her only girl.

"And this is Julian," their dad adds, shifting their youngest
to his other arm as if he weighs nothing at all.

"Arthur is excited to join the band this year," his mother
continues. "He already plays the violin."

"Wonderful!" I've been waiting for this, and I'm ready with
my advice if they are ready to hear it.

"This might sound surprising," I say to Arthur, "but I think
trombone might be perfect for you. You can put your skills for
finding notes on the violin strings to use on the trombone
slide. Plus, most of the other students will be learning to read
music for the first time. If you have to learn to read a new clef

you will continue to be challenged, and you'll know two clefs in the end—a good skill for potential piano players."

A week later, Arthur and his two best buddies (both redheads) arrive at the band room door for their first small-group trombone lesson. Principal Hawkins follows them through the door and gets settled with her laptop in the corner for the first of my three yearly observations. The boys take their seats in front of trombones labeled neatly in my handwriting with their names.

"Welcome to Lesson One! Our first task is to learn which side of the case is the top, so your instrument doesn't come flying out each time you try to open it."

They look at the cases incredulously. Principal Hawkins looks up from her notes as well. It's not my first rodeo anymore, and with one lighthearted sentence I've led them around one potential pothole.

"Your instruments are very excited to meet you," I add with a smile.

I am instantly met with the same lightheartedness I give them. Together we discover the top of the case by the serial number I have written there, and with more enduring methods, like the way the latches work smoothly under your fingers when the case is right side up.

"Now you know what to look for," I encourage. "Everything has a trick. You just have to find it."

The clicks of cases opening radiate through the band room. It is one of my favorite sounds, our blank canvas of possibility. They lay their cases open on the floor.

"Now find the mouthpiece," I say, showing them mine. "It's often tucked in a smaller compartment to keep it from hitting the other sections of your trombone."

They each find theirs, and together we buzz our first tones

in front of the compact mirrors I've placed on their flimsy folding stands. Once they have successfully made their first sound on the mouthpiece and understand its use in tone production, we learn about the other pieces of the trombone and where they fit in. Piece by piece we assemble their new sidekicks with steps that will soon be familiar, while their cases remain splayed open at their feet.

As I check their work, I ask a playful question—one I enjoy using to get to know my new students.

"What will you name them?"

One redhead has his answer immediately.

"Einstein," he says with a self-assured nod.

"Kobe," adds the other competitively, his side smile filling the pause that precedes the last answer.

Arthur thoughtfully examines his new companion. I am not sure what he's doing but he turns the trombone over in his hands and squints at the engravings on its bell. The others peer over to see if he has found what he's looking for. He has. It already has a perfect name etched there under the emblem of a crown. All he needs to do is say it.

"King," he quotes quietly.

"Perfect," I reply to them all.

I help them balance the trombones on their shoulders, and the redheads pretend they are telescopes while I get Arthur situated. He holds it like he's done this before. He's a natural. Then we make the first sounds together, and they laugh at themselves. But I can see they're hooked. Each of their attempts reveals improvement and the impressive aptitude of each one.

I show them how to clean, disassemble, and pack up just as deliberately. Then those fearless fourth graders leave, proudly wielding their new instruments, ready to share the raucous joy of beginner band with their families until our next lesson.

"You left no stone unturned," Mrs. Hawkins says to me after the lesson concludes.

"Well, I suppose it's the kindergarten of band," I say, trying to relate it to her more intimately known world of early childhood education and remedial reading.

"Yes," she replies. "Everything is important in the beginning, because absolutely anything is possible from here."

Where the Valley Widens

"MY NAME IS MRS. OAKS. And I am going to tell you about this place."

I'm grateful for the break. Sweat drips down my back, and my calves are complaining louder than the students as we arrive at the seventeen-foot white marble obelisk at the top of the hill. Every spring, the fifth graders learn local history, and this year I am a chaperone on the highly anticipated historic walking tour. We've finally herded the fifth graders up the steep path of Evergreen Cemetery for this lesson on the Valley.

"This monument," Mrs. Oaks tells us, "is for a Mohawk maiden who was a Christian missionary, and an educational patron for her people." Tired from the walk, and already impressed by her aura, every student in the fifth grade falls silent.

"This obelisk stands for something beautiful that we lost too soon. She was only twenty-one when she died in a tragic train accident. The people of The Valley erected this monument three years later in 1855. It is the earliest known monument to a Native American woman in the United States."

Mrs. Oaks gestures to the view behind her and continues.

"If you have not already felt it, there is power in this place." The trees are sparse here at this higher elevation, and we all take in the view of the Valley. Its expanse opens before us, the river at its center.

She tells us the Haudenosaunee word for this spot means *Where the Valley Widens*. "They named this land," she says, "for the way her oak-covered hills break open for winter snow melts and upland streams to drain into the river."

I can see the sweat seeping through the shirts of the students in front of me, but they are captivated.

"Generals James Clinton and John Sullivan's armies took the valley in 1779. By 1786 settlers founded the town, finding its fields could grow cows and crops equally well. They built a railroad junction and summer ferries to the river's Big Island, which still teems with flora, fauna, and local lore in just as much abundance." A light breeze shifts the leaves and cools our sweaty faces as she goes on. "In autumn, you can see the hickory, maple, and beech trees streaking the hills with colors as vibrant as those on historic mansions and artisan shops that line our village streets...."

All summer, with Mrs. Oaks' words still in my mind, I notice more of the Valley's magic. Murders of crows cross my path, as they wake from safe city sleeps to answer the call of the countryside. The highway hugs the river that leads me to the village there. Great sycamores attend the entire journey, while my traveling companions shift from darting city crows to perched suburban hawks. Occasionally, a lone bald eagle or great blue heron will soar across the sky as daylight and my silver sedan break through the mists that rise off the river and its marshlands. I always feel encouraged when I see them.

Today, a heron greets me overhead as I turn off the

highway, onto the bridge that leads to the town square. There the main road divides around a burnt brick courthouse, with a quartet of limestone-trimmed turrets. I learned from Mrs. Oaks that it has overseen the village's comings and goings since 1871. My earliest memories of the village are from a childhood visit to enjoy a gazebo puppet show and picnic on the courthouse lawn. This has always been a good place to raise a family. And family is one reason I've returned to it.

I remember my mother directing my wandering attention to the scene on the stage, but I was enchanted by the trickle of a forgotten fountain supporting a painted iron fireman. He cradled a child in one arm and lifted a lantern with the other. He stood alone, like a lighthouse, protecting the power of this place and the ocean of histories only he remembered. The stage's lines and lyrics faded for me beneath the possibilities of this statue's story. What did he see from way up there? What was he looking for? Everything about him was a mystery to me.

I still wonder these things as I pass him now on my drive to school. He is falling into disrepair, but I still feel a kinship with him, as though somehow we are protecting the same precious thing. I place a hand on my growing belly and imagine the beauty he could bring back to the heart of the village if he were repaired.

I enter the parking lot with the creek on my left and rows of birch trees before me. Today I am moving out of my first classroom, which looks east over unruly yew bushes and bus lanes.

In an effort to create more coherent primary and intermediate wings, the band and music rooms are both being moved to the center hallway next to the art room for next year. I am excited to be near Miss Clay (and the faculty room bathroom, now that I have my own little one on the way), but

I am also sad to leave the walls that hold my first teaching memories.

After a morning of work, I am drenched in sweat. Dan and my parents bring lunch and help me set up. Moving the entire band room while pregnant has my nesting instincts in high gear, and all the changes have me feeling like I'm starting all over. The schedule will also shift with the new school year to accommodate important intervention initiatives. Making it work is going to require creative problem solving on my part. As Dan and my parents stock the shelves with the larger instruments, I sit at my desk trying to work on the schedule through the fog of pregnancy and the heat of summer's last days.

My second classroom looks north, toward the secondary school and the expanse of athletic fields between them. Even though I miss my old room and the ease of its predictable schedule, I try to appreciate the even wider view of the Valley I have here. My fourth year starts in a room that doesn't feel like home yet. The fourth graders don't miss the old room because they never knew it, but the fifth graders seem more nostalgic and miffed over the change than I am.

Autumn comes, and so does my maternity leave. This time as a new family goes too quickly. I cherish every second and even bring my new baby boy, Rhyse, to visit the folks at school on my last day of leave in late January.

My fourth and fifth graders ogle him like a herd of grandmas.

"Oh," Lynn Finch squeals. "He's so cute!"

He smiles up at her.

"You have a way with babies," I say.

"He's getting so big!"

"Where does the time go!"

"I bet you're gonna miss this little man."

"Piffle," scoffs Mrs. Darling at their remarks, which they have obviously picked up from their parents. She gives me a big hug.

"Nice job, Mama," she says.

Returning is tough. Everyone cries their first day back, and I am no exception. But it helps that students and teachers alike seem excited to have me again. Lessons and rehearsals are rocky because I've been away, so most of my joy comes from students who visit the new room to practice if they have completed all their classwork. Most arrive during their recess or in the morning as buses trickle in and their peers meander through the breakfast line. In these hollows of the master schedule, squeezed between mandated interventions, we get our best work done.

"Ugh!" The door slams open unceremoniously. "I'm gonna barf from my bus ride." A shapeless book bag slides across my new room's floor like a hockey puck. The arms of a coat are still through its straps when it lands in the corner by our new Scout-made riser. Ella flops down in the nearest folding chair and assembles her clarinet in seconds.

"Why? Was it a bumpy drive?" I inquire.

"Nah, my driver's the best," she says, tying her dirty blond hair back in a ponytail. "Let's just say we all know Eli had beans for dinner last night."

"Ah, I see. Any other news from the morning route?"

"Nah, only that I'm gonna quit tomorrow." Ella moves the reed in her mouth with her tongue as she talks, just one of her many endearing talents.

Her untied laces, wet with February slush, lie limp across the floor as she opens her dog-eared lesson book. Its pages are as gray as her laces.

"I can't play 'Aura Lee.' I'm gonna have to quit." She places her reed on her mouthpiece with surprising precision, while straightening her back to perfect playing position on the front edge of her chair. Before I can say anything that might be helpful, she has transformed. She works her own enchantments on "Aura Lee" with the steady strokes a fairy godmother might use to transform Cinderella into a princess.

I type a quick email to her classroom teacher: *She's here. I'll send her to math lab after the Pledge.* Apparently, Ella is a handful everywhere else she goes, so a morning practice session while the other buses arrive is better for everyone involved. It gets her focused for her newly scheduled math interventions, which are overseen by Mr. Goras.

I straighten up the chairs while other students drop off their instruments in our new cubbies before heading to breakfast and homeroom. Then I begin writing the day's objectives on the smartboard that has replaced last year's whiteboard, which had replaced the chalkboard I began with just three years ago. This past summer during the move, an Eagle Scout made us trumpet risers, a music cabinet, and my first real podium. To match his efforts, the school's carpenter installed instrument shelving around the perimeter of the entire space. My new room is amazing, updated, and organized, but it doesn't feel like home. Not yet.

Completely focused, Ella finally forgets about whatever Eli had for dinner last night and the person she is outside this room. I place a metronome on her stand. "Ugh!" is her only reply before continuing on to discover its power. It leads her through her morning practice session like a horse-drawn carriage on its way to Cinderella's ball. But of course, the clock must always strike midnight, or in this case, 9:00 AM. In what feels like an instant, her fifteen minutes at the ball are up.

Beep!

"Good morning! Please stand for the Pledge of Allegiance."

As we stand and recite the spell, I imagine myself saying it on my deathbed instead of "Our Father...," due to pure repetition and the degradation of advanced age. With the bell, Ella is transfigured back to her previously frazzled self, and she packs up in the same whirlwind she arrived in.

"Ugh, Mr. Goras is gonna kill me. I have no idea what I'm doing. I'm terrible at math, and I've lost my pencil again."

I hand her a black Ticonderoga No. 2 as I open the door and say, "Have a good day. See you at your lesson."

She rolls her eyes, her backpack falling off one shoulder as she grabs the pencil.

"You know I'm gonna quit tomorrow," she confirms as she stumbles out the door, nearly colliding with Anne's little brother James, who must be running an errand for his teacher.

"I know," I say with a smile to myself and to him. James and I watch Ella meet her math teacher a few doors down. Mr. Goras offers a wave of reciprocity, which I return in kind as James sneaks a silent glance at the drums in the band room.

Tomorrow we will repeat the same ritual, just as we did every day last year in my room around the corner, and just as we will every day that remains of this year. The new room feels like the old one when she is in it. It feels like ours. Her accidental magic holds power over this place. Every day she tells me she is quitting, and every day we enjoy each other's company, pretending not to know what the next day brings. At the end of the year, when she comes to say goodbye, despite myself I feel the impact of her masked dedication. When I tell her homeroom teacher so, she just laughs in disbelief. Apparently, she doesn't believe in magic.

Ella will end up quitting—in middle school—just like she told me she would. And I will have no idea if she ever plays again. But it won't matter. She's shown me how to love a thing you know is leaving and let it live its numbered days unfettered by expectation—or anything at all. By the end, when she says, "I'm quitting tomorrow," I know she really means, "I played to share today with you," and therein lies the power of this place.

Like the heron and the statue, she and I, and occasionally others, reward each other with a great and unintended magic. It wells where we walk and flows from the intersection of our paths, which is the only place Where the Valley Widens for any of us.

YEAR FOUR

"If you can keep your head when all about you
Are losing theirs and blaming it on you;"

From *If*
by Rudyard Kipling

Graduation

ALONG WITH MY SECOND ROOM comes the second Finch. Even though the same conditions exist for her to choose trombone like her brother, Lynn has chosen flute. And that matters.

In February, after my maternity leave, she learns it methodically in a lesson group of raffish personalities. Her class is one to be remembered, and one every teacher talks about with trepidation. These young people shatter all norms. They extirpate mandated modules, leaving a trail of terrifying state test scores in their wake. Their common core belief is obvious: What they don't want to do, they don't do; and what they want to do gets done.

The band is no better. Maybe it's because I was out on leave; maybe it's the new-parent sleep deprivation, or all the changes in our school environment. But whatever the reason, I am once again doubting my abilities as a teacher. I leave countless rehearsals wrung out, convinced I'm not meant for this profession. *How could I be?*

With every incident that arises, I question myself and suffer greatly for my indecision. Students sense my openness and exploit it as much as possible. I know my approach is not working. But I don't enjoy micromanaging anyone or writing permission slips to go pee, like the band room's Lord of the Lavatory.

My previous insecurities are dwarfed by the misgivings that arise with this group. I dread the whirlwind of our rehearsals from the moment I hear their wild stampede pounding down the hallway. "Whack-a-Mole" is the best way to describe the havoc that ensues for the next twenty-eight minutes. All progress halts at their wall of incessant chatter and derailing questions. Every one of their erratic inquiries commences with "Mswilliams..." and a wild hand wave in my general direction. These beginner bandsmen are experts in contriving chaos. They obliterate my ability to think and make me shudder at the sound of my own name.

The pre-rehearsal "warm up" is a cacophony of these ruffians testing the breaking point of sound, their instruments, and my patience. The unified attempts we do make only vaguely resemble the patterns one might recognize as music. However, their playing is my best and only escape from the unending racket their swinging feet produce against the metal bars of our folding chairs and stands. At the conclusion of rehearsal, the anarchy of packing up quickly dissolves any relief I might have imagined. Then I am left alone in the aftermath of their wreckage thinking, *Why is this so hard?*

I weave through the jumble of scattered chairs and stands, which they have hastily ejected in all directions in their great race out the door. I straighten their seats, and collect name tags, smashed pencils, and crumpled sheet music covered in doodles off the floor. It is my quiet second Finch sitting patiently through March rehearsals, waiting for me to figure it out, who inspires me to press ahead. I know I cannot let her down. This is her one chance at a great fourth-grade year. There has to be a trick. I just need to find it.

So, out of necessity, I begin to modify the traditional rehearsal structure I was educated in and have used with my previous classes. I read more of Frank Battisti's books, and in lessons I start asking, "What did you notice?" Then I let them choose the problems we tackle. With curiosity, I play along with them at every step on every instrument, to gain the empathy of experience I lack. I become a scientist of my students and unintentionally model more of the things I value. As April approaches, their tornado of destruction starts morphing into one of excitement, curiosity, and creativity. Slowly I am gaining poise and intuition, like a musical Mary Poppins.

Although we do not get as far in our lesson book this year, we do other things. Students who need to talk take on the daily announcements, speaking for me whenever possible. Eventually they will introduce the pieces at our concert. Kids who want to move set up chairs and stands. Folks who doodle in the margins of their music are tasked with sketching scenes to project during our performance. Finally, we string together our concert songs with a skit written by the same fingers that struggle through their scales. The band begins to feel like one big Odyssey of the Mind team, and it suits them.

At the June concert, students act out their skit to a backdrop of their own artwork and the soundtrack of their band songs. It is fresh, and it delights the parents along with the younger siblings who have been dragged there. We've created a mini-masterpiece, and although our rehearsals are still messy, the concert is magnificent.

It has taken me a while, but I am beginning to figure it out. I can see it in Lynn's eyes.

And that matters.

I did it for her just as much as I did it for myself. I did it to survive. But parents and principals alike praise our spring concert more than ever. If their technical level is lower, it is of little importance to families who want their children to learn to believe in themselves from a teacher who does too. This year, I learn that each class teaches you the lesson you need next.

As the end of June creeps closer, with our concerts complete, we take our last rehearsals out to the field by the band room to learn marching basics in the heat. We share our final morning lessons beneath shady trees, treating our brass instruments to deeply needed baths in shallow trays of clean water. Eleven-year-old hands join my own in cleaning off the crud of another year. "This is my favorite lesson of all," I hear over and over as we prepare the instruments for next year's crew, which now always includes some siblings. It is one of my favorite lessons too.

A few weeks later, as the year draws to a close, Miss Clay announces her marriage and corresponding move to be with her new husband. So when fifth graders and their families assemble in the gym for the graduation ceremony, I feel that she is graduating too. Beneath the basketball hoops, the superintendent recounts the students' accomplishments and the middle school principal welcomes them to their new school. Finally, the fifth-grade teachers call their students up one by one, names booming through the microphone and ricocheting off the walls of the gymnasium. Each student parades to the front to receive their diploma in larger versions of shoes they learned to tie right there.

The ceremony concludes with a slideshow of each student's fifth grade photograph, followed by one from kindergarten. The daily growth that was difficult to see is now immediately evident with the help of time's gracious hand and photographic evidence. "Oooh's" and "Aww's" and laughter rise in waves through the crowd, and we all stay afterward sharing stories, soda, and cupcakes.

Once the families have dispersed, the remaining staff members toast paper cups of orange soda to Miss Clay and our retirees. We rack the folding chairs, while veteran teachers reminisce about teaching alongside their long-retired colleagues. I see the way the ones who are leaving listen. Do they wonder what stories we will tell about them when they are gone?

They laugh now at scenarios that once boiled their blood as we pack up leftover cupcakes to take to the custodial crew. "Those were the Dark Ages, and we didn't all make it," they agree, and the conversations soon return to brighter stories of students and staff that still make them smile: Green eggs and ham from the kitchen staff on April Fool's Day. The year the PT and OT staff dressed up like Cinderella characters and "transformed" a student's wheelchair into a princess carriage.

Their stories remind me of the many beautiful scenes I've witnessed too. Just last year, Arthur Finch fell seriously ill, and his friends were so worried about him that we wrote him letters in our lessons instead of practicing our scales. When he finally returned to school, it was with an IV of antibiotics and a smile as big as ever. His red-headed buddies attended to his every need, overjoyed to have him back. Their kinship tugged on the heartstrings of all the adults who knew them. Reliving these moments, especially after the trials and triumphs of a year with a class-like-no-other, makes me feel like I am graduating too.

In our last two days, with the students already on summer break, we tidy our rooms, covering bookcases and hauling furniture to the halls for the yearly waxing of the floors.

Becky's radio blares Alice Cooper's "School's Out for Summer" and teachers use intercom codes to broadcast unnecessary announcements in each other's rooms. The few young teachers, myself still included, are the main recipients of this happy hazing because without the cipher we are helpless to retaliate. Still, we embrace the game with the taste of summer's elation sweet on our lips.

In my room, I place cleaned instruments in handcrafted cubbies, and I inventory everything in a tidy digital spreadsheet as the clothespin on my computer and the poem on my wall keep me company.

I file the year's music and place our new black folders in the Scout-made music rack by the door. Finally, I place the year's concert programs in a file and a handful of student thank-you cards in a brimming folder right beside it. Soon I'll really need that box. I've been so busy surviving that I haven't gotten one yet, but I know the notes are safe in my desk drawer. This fall when I visit Lonnie's shop, I'll pick one up.

At last, I step back to survey the room. Everything is in its place. It only took four years, but I finally have my head above water. After stumbling through being a new teacher and a new mom, moving rooms, and attempting to find myself on and off the podium, I finally feel like I am ready for this job. It wasn't what I expected, but I've finally chosen it.

And that matters.

I close the band room door to hear the clanging of assorted dishes under running water across the hall in our lunchroom. Through the doorway I see Becky and Miss Clay, trading stories just to hear each other laugh over what others might see as chores. As I walk to my car, I recall the veteran teachers' anecdotes of both bright and dark ages. These are the allegories my sibling survivors have chosen to tell me. And that matters too. I leave the year feeling that, despite the difficulty, this is the right kind of lesson and the right kind of weary. As my feet leave the lines of the crosswalk for my car, an insistent train horn blares a block away, and I know, even now, that today is one of the good old days.

Largo

Year 5 - 7

*"And if ever I should meet you, by land or by sea,
I will always remember your kindness to me."*

~Irish Song

YEAR FIVE

"If you can trust yourself when all men doubt you,
But make allowance for their doubting too;"

~Rudyard Kipling

Rain

TODAY IS MY *FIFTH* FIRST DAY OF SCHOOL. I don my first-day clothes and the chance to start again, doing it differently from Day One with all that I've learned. I pull out of my driveway and into my year, embracing this beautiful beginning. It's like any other first day—except for the rain. I start my wipers and the radio too.

"Goooooood morning, this is your hometown station, WTVW, and that was Bob Dylan's 'Hard Rain's A-Gonna Fall,'" the DJ announces.

"Speaking of rain, Dave," his cohost chimes in, "we are receiving some wet weather out there. Make sure to grab those umbrellas! We're getting pummeled with what remains of tropical storm Lee today, the thirteenth named storm of the season. Its winds are petering out, but you can expect nothing but rain for the next few days."

I turn off the radio. It rained last week too.

Yesterday the staff met and told sad tales of too-short summers. We added finishing touches to our rooms and stepped back to admire the handiwork of our countless summer hours. Welcome banners hung above doorways, and happy little name tags adorned student desks and cubbies, waiting for the children we would meet today. When we left yesterday, we felt "as ready as we'll ever be!"

I arrive and dart from the staff parking lot to the school's side door, trying to keep my first-day dress dry. Buses pull up and students pour into the building between raindrops, wearing spiffy backpacks stuffed with fresh school supplies. But they've hardly begun unloading their gear and organizing their desks when a steady stream of phone calls and pickups begin. Parents speak in hushed tones to Mrs. DuBois. They have all come for the same reason.

"The river is rising," they whisper.

Teachers attempt to continue their welcome rituals, but Dr. Seuss read-alouds are interrupted again and again by intercom calls from Mrs. Ferri. This year, in place of ice breakers, teachers learn their students' names as they are called to the office to leave early.

By the time the emergency dismissal is announced, only about a hundred of our five hundred students remain. This is the only time we've ever used the emergency procedures we practice each fall. There is a surreal sense of calm within the situation. We know what to do since we've done it so many times. Yet this is the first time it's real. Students and new staff follow the veterans' lead and their collective knowledge, but in truth these are uncharted waters for all of us.

What's left of each class enters the gym and goes to their usual assembly spots. However, there is no Code of Conduct Meeting or Welcome Celebration. Instead, one hundred children follow their teachers in strangely silent lines to their places under bleak basketball hoops on this first day of school. Lynn Finch searches for Julian across the cavernous gymnasium, and they silently confirm one another's disquiet. Julian is in third grade now, but I think of our first day with

Mrs. Darling when I see him. Today, five first days later, we are suddenly just as unsure as we were back then.

Forced to take alternate routes to get to us, buses come out of order. The arrival of each one is quickly documented by its number in black dry-erase marker on the gym wall's whiteboard. The only sound is the hum of fluorescent lights, interrupted by a singular voice announcing bus numbers and names for pickup. The special education team ferries students out the door and to their parents, accounting for every single child.

Then, without warning, another announcement: *"If you live out of town, you must go now."*

Even amidst the emergency, the cadence reminds me of the refrain from an old Dr. Seuss book: "Marvin K. Mooney, will you please go now!" It seems absurd that this crosses my mind at this moment, but it is insistent. School is a safe place for stories and predictable patterns. Today the stories are on the shelves, and we are living something much more real.

The school has volunteers to stay until all the students are home. So like Marvin, I go.

I leave everything in my room untouched. There is not a second to spare for packing up. *It's all first-day tidy anyway,* I reassure myself on my way out the door. If I don't go now, the roads might become impassable, and I could be stuck in this gym overnight.

The fishbowl entranceway is still packed with parents, but the line out the door is gone. Mrs. Ferri is still answering the phone, and Mrs. DuBois is pairing the last of the guardians with their children. Both women are calm for the kids, hiding their worry with their work, but neither has seen a day like today.

Outside, the sky is black and bearish. Relentless sheets hammer the roofs of the cars in the parking lot, and I am soaked in seconds. On my drive, I'm redirected off my usual route and away from the underpass, which is already quickly filling with water. I join a line of evacuating motorists, diverted again and again by an adept team of emergency service workers who know the only clear path to the expressway. We finally reach the highway to find the river creeping over its edges at its lowest points. It will be submerged soon. I've never seen it like this before.

I think through all possible routes home as I drive, in case we are diverted again. Our options are quickly disappearing, as we are all funneled onto the only routes left. I know our caravan must stretch nearly all the way home, but there is so much rain and road spray I can barely see the car in front of me.

The rain is so loud, I can't hear the radio. It is just a running list of early dismissals and flood warnings anyway—news I already know. When I get off the freeway, I see road closures, detours, and emergency service vehicles everywhere. Water is pooling in unusual places. As I pass the hospital, their newly installed floodgates are rising from the ground in a race against the river—a race, I fear, that has no winner.

Night falls early, and it is still raining as I tell my one-year-old Rhyse the stories we should have heard today. Then I sing him to sleep while our first-day-of-school rituals recede under a sky without stars. My dreams return to the rain and the river, repeating like a mantra in my mind. Nightmares siphon my sleep, but I cannot stop them, and when I wake it is to the sound of rushing water.

Rivers

DAN AND I STUMBLE DOWN THE STAIRS and splash into the six inches of water covering our entire cellar floor. We are dumbfounded. We look around frantically at the shelves for something that can help. They are packed with equipment Dan has acquired, mostly second-hand, for all his home hobbies, which mostly involve fermenting sourdough bread, yogurt, and wine.

In seconds, Dan has grabbed a pump he bought for his recent foray into home brewing. He sets it up in the laundry room, pumping water from the floor into a utility sink on the side wall. I dump bucket after bucket in as well. We pump water out of the basement all night long as it pours in through an old coal shoot in an unending, raging waterfall. I worry about how tired I will be at school the next day, but we can't stop. Two floors above, Rhyse sleeps soundly while we tread water in the cellar.

I'll never forget the sickening sound of it. If we didn't have the pump, if we'd lost power, if one more thing had gone wrong, we would have lost our furnace, washer, dryer, electrical box, Dan's collection of gadgets—not to mention the less expensive but more priceless boxes of memories we stored down there. But our power stayed on, and although we lost a night's sleep, we didn't lose anything else.

The next morning, we awake bleary from our interrupted slumber to the hum of helicopters in the sky and a sinking sadness for our neighbors who have lost all the things we didn't. I've expected a call from our phone tree to tell me school is canceled, but I haven't gotten one yet. I try calling my parents, but the lines are down—probably the reason I haven't heard anything from the school. So I turn on my radio and wait to hear the list of cancellations. My regular station barely comes through.

"This is Dave from WTVW." A scratchy voice fights through the static. "We are broadcasting from a camper at our AM tower site because of river flooding in our area. If you are just tuning in, the Southern Tier is in a state of emergency. Both the Susquehanna and the Chenango Rivers have breached their banks..." His voice cuts in and out as he lists areas that have been evacuated and where the closest shelters have been set up. Soon I lose the station's reception entirely, but I've learned what I need to know for now.

Everything is canceled. Apparently, my neighborhood is a thankful little island, surrounded by the muddy waters of our twin flooded rivers.

With everything called off and nowhere to go, Dan and I put Rhyse in his carrier and walk the neighborhood. We don't get far. A block away we find houses sitting in the river, with only their second floors peeking out above the waterline like abandoned boats. Some neighbors are actively emptying the Susquehanna from their homes with buckets and hoses. It feels too invasive to be here at such a painful moment, and since we don't know how to help, we head back home to the sound of pumps and running water everywhere.

It wasn't even a hurricane. Just some tropical storm. But the teachers who live by the river knew yesterday. They whispered it to each other and into their phones during early dismissal: "Yes, move it all. I'll be home soon." Those families from the flats who had come early for their children in a stream as steady as the rain knew it too. They knew, but there was nothing they could do to stop the storm.

I try to call and check on Becky, but the phone lines are still down. All day, there is no news from my downstream school's little town, but I don't need the news to tell me what their worried faces all told me yesterday. Everything is underwater. Our ship is sinking.

On the third day, the rivers recede. There is a brown shadow everywhere, reminding us where the water once was. The radio confirms another day of no school. I try the phone again, and it's working. I call my parents and Becky. They have water in their basements, but otherwise they are okay. No one has heard about the school yet.

Dan and I spend the day cleaning our basement and emptying dehumidifiers in the utility sink. We still can't go anywhere, so after I put Rhyse to bed, I turn on our PC to see if we have internet yet. We do. My searches and social media feed show shot after shot of the sadness, most taken by photographers in the helicopters we've been hearing. Through my screen I see streets and sidewalks ending in water, freeways and houses covered in seas of mud. From a bird's eye view, I witness the wreckage of every city, village, and town in the tri-county area.

I am about to sign off when I begin to see photos of the Valley. They too are all aerial, since the only way in and out of my school's small town is by boat. I see homes, shops, and churches filled with water. And finally, the photo I have been searching for and hoping not to see: our little elementary school, surrounded by those brooding waters. She is lost at sea, her treasures sunken, her crew all castaways. My heart breaks.

"Dan," I call quietly down the stairs, "come see this." I tell myself I'm being dramatic as I hear his footsteps on the stairs.

"Oh, no," is all he says when he sees it.

"Maybe the water only came to the edges of the school." I try zooming in on the photo, but I can't tell. I feel anxiety rising in my chest. "If there is water in the school, what happens next?"

"I don't know," he replies.

"Are all the instruments ruined? Just like that?" He only looks at me with a sorry expression as I attempt to quell my emotions with reason. "The woodwinds might not be salvageable, but I bet the brass could be professionally sanitized."

"Maybe..." His voice trails off, but I can tell he doesn't think that's going to happen.

"My instruments are there too. I'll be able to get them, right?" I have one of each instrument I teach. In addition to the ones I've had since the beginning, each year I've saved up and purchased another as a birthday present to myself so I can play along with the students.

"Oh, I hope so," he says, squeezing my shoulder.

What if all I've been working for is destroyed? I think. But I can't ask that question out loud yet. I don't want it to be real.

My mind is working now, trying to make sense of what I see. "If all the instruments are totaled, what does that mean about the school? It's not ruined too, right?" Dan just puts his arm around me. "And if it is—which hopefully it isn't—I'll at least get a chance to gather my things and say goodbye to my room, right?"

"It's too soon to tell," he says. "But I hope so. Either way I think we have a long road ahead of us."

My mind turns in circles over the photo, and seeing I am making no progress, Dan shuts off the screen. But it doesn't matter. The image stays in front of my eyes, and a sinking feeling stays in my stomach as I head to bed. Neither one of us knows what this really means, but I do know that Where the Valley Widens, the river does too.

Rock Bottom

THEY CALL US IN FOR A MEETING on the fourth day, telling us the one passable route we can use. Firemen and armed policemen monitor it, letting only residents, emergency crews, and now us through. It feels like a war zone. Piles of flood-damaged everything are everywhere, lining the streets like plowed snow after a blizzard. Carpets, furniture, photos, toys. *Every single house*. Every family is walking from their home to their ever-growing heap, again and again, soaked in river water, with armloads of memories caked in silty mud.

As we drive through the neighborhood near the schools' shared campus, we pass a great piece of particle board fashioned into a makeshift sign. Red spray-painted capital letters spell out: **You loot. We shoot.**

The district staff assembles in the high school gymnasium. Just one field away, this building was spared. Many of us are missing. In the eerie glow of the emergency lights, Mr. O'Dell begins.

"There were four and a half feet of water in the elementary school, the district office, and the maintenance building."

Silence.

"There is also some damage to the new middle school and high school."

Silence.

"And it was not just river water that was in our schools. It was farm runoff. Creek water infused with animal waste, refuse, and gasoline from all the flooded farm machinery and vehicles in the area. Our buildings, and everything in them, are a total loss. No one is allowed in, and nothing is coming out. Thankfully," he adds, "a neighboring district has offered to rent us an empty building and we will begin setting up tomorrow."

With those words, any hope we have of salvaging something of our lives there is lost. That's when they lose it. A strained voice cries out, "How can you do this? We can't come in tomorrow!"

It's Mr. Goras. Anger seethes through his teeth.

"We've lost everything. Our homes, our churches, everything. Our grandparents, our cousins, our neighbors have lost everything. It's not just this school. You're not from here. You'll never understand."

Mr. Goras collapses on the shoulder of Mrs. Darling sitting beside him, trying to hide his tears. She puts her arm around him.

He is right. We breathe for a beat. Mr. O'Dell was not trained for this.

"Of course, if you need to be at home, that is where you must go." Mr. O'Dell knows his next words already. "Take care of your families, your neighbors, and yourselves first. We will take care of those of you who are caring for others. Those of us who can will come set up tomorrow."

The loss of the locals is just so immense. The meeting is over, and people begin leaving, along with any last hopes I had that the photos were somehow misleading.

We've arrived at absolute zero. Our beautiful elementary school ecosystem has been shattered by mother nature's fury. We have nothing but each other, and the inequity of fate strains even that. The group disperses in all directions through various gym doors. Neighbors return to the painful work of purging their past. With arms around each other, they process in mud-covered boots to their homes and heavy heaps.

It will be months of disinfecting and demolition before recovery and rebuilding can even begin. Becky and Mrs. Marion hug by the bleachers, and the fourth-grade teachers speak in quiet tones, hoping their pain will be less harrowing if they say it softer. The gym feels like a funeral parlor as we greet each other in grief.

I hear the other teachers talking.

"Even if they can get us supplies, all our curriculum was in there," says Mrs. Marion.

"None of mine was digital," says Mrs. Darling.

"How are we supposed to teach without it?" adds Mr. Goras.

All our work is ruined. Our collective knowledge is gone. I am realizing that the instruments, and the main achievements of my first four years of teaching, are also gone. Thankfully, I took that big red binder home for summer lesson planning and forgot to bring it back. Now it's the only thing from the school I have left.

I don't know what to do or where to go. I am about to leave when I see Mr. F heading toward me. His excellence and renown have only increased since my first demo day, and I've spent all of my first four years here remaining intimidated by him. Until now, I've only known the impressive part of him that he wants the world to see—a strong and fearless leader. But that is not the man who walks toward me now.

We all have our own pain, but I can see, in this moment, that he knows mine acutely. He takes me under his wing and back to his room, since I have none. The tears I've held back till now trickle down my face as we silently walk the darkened hallways. When we get to his room, he hands me a tissue and we tell each other how our families are doing. Both our houses sit on little islands of luck, surrounded by the waters of our flooded neighborhoods. We mourn for our friends and neighbors who have lost so much more.

Then we share the loss of the fruits of my first four years, all those instruments and the hours it took to retrieve and repair them. Our new tuba and bass clarinet. That old, painted bass drum. All the cases with layers of masking-taped name tags, which have—until now—immortalized its lineage of previous players. The music library with its handwritten director notes, mimeograph copies, and recently modernized repertoire. The tidy files of concert programs covered in student artwork and photographs of glorious bands gone by. All of it lost, along with the memories they carried, which far outdate me and even Mr. F.

My own instruments, diplomas, teaching certificates, and family photos are in there too. They're on the walls with my poem and in the bottom drawer of my desk along with the file folder that was the beginning of my box. Professional and personal are inseparable now, all unsalvageable.

I can still taste my tears when he tells me the plan. *How does he have a plan?* I listen. I have no other choice. I have nothing and I know nothing. My mind is blank. I cannot think. There is too much to do. Where do we even start? Everything I thought I knew has been washed away with all the things I've worked for. My thoughts drift from the steady canter of his voice.

How can I possibly be a band director with no school, no

93

instruments, no music? How can families even think about music when they are homeless? This year was supposed to be easier. Why is this so hard?

I want to slam my fists down on the desk, but I don't. I'm angry that I let myself care so much about this. He looks at me through his round glasses, and as if in response to my thoughts, he answers, "You might not feel like this is true right now, but it is times like these when we need music the most." I clench my teeth tightly. I don't believe him, but I want to.

Mr. F has always been there, taking care of our department across the campus and observing my novice progress, but now we are linked. Linked because he can see a path I cannot. Linked because I need him, even though I don't know it. Linked in the silent disappointment that this is it: Life and teaching are really this hard. They've always been and will continue to be. My freight's been filled with water and washed away. I feel as though I'm going nowhere and that the world just wants me to give up.

And it could have been that way. It is for many others.

But Mr. F has other plans for me, and it is in this moment that I accept him as my teacher for the first time. He drags me along with the drive of a powerful locomotive. He knows where we are going and how to get there because this is not the first time he has transformed misfortune into motion. Nor will it be the last. This is just the first time we go together.

From our meeting this morning, we know that kindergarten through fourth grade will be in the rented school down the road, but the fifth grade will come to this building, a shared sixth- through twelfth-grade campus.

"Listen," he says, "the middle school band director and I will clear an old equipment shelf for the fifth-grade instruments. We will get donations. We will lend you things." He grabs a lined legal pad and makes two bulleted to-do lists.

"We will move our desks out of the office so it can be a lesson room for your fifth graders. I'll take care of getting you a computer and desk, and we will make a schedule that incorporates the fifth-grade band rehearsals into the middle school band room's daily schedule." He hands me another tissue and one manageable to-do list. "Tomorrow you'll set up the fourth-grade band at the other school, and then we'll go one day at a time."

He puts a hand on my shoulder. "We'll get back on track."

As I drive away, I stop at the first house with people out front. It turns out to be the home of our school speech pathologist. I open my trunk to give her family cases of bottled water, non-perishable food, and cleaning supplies that I picked up before coming. As I drive away, I see her and her husband share a much-needed water break in my rearview mirror, their three kids digging into the freshly delivered granola bars on their soggy front steps. I return my gaze to the road before me, but looking forward is just as hard as looking back. So instead, I listen, just like Mr. F told me to, finding what little comfort is left to me in the familiar sound of my wheels rumbling over the railroad tracks.

Ashes

EVEN THOUGH THE DRIVE TO OUR NEW SCHOOL begins the same way, it all feels different. Instead of trekking to my little rural village, I exit earlier and snake through the small city there. I pass what remains of my parents' outsourced industries and numerous fast-food restaurants, until the urban sidewalks give way to a country road that I follow for a quarter of a mile. Snuggled between a neighborhood grocery store and an aromatic chicken barbecue joint is our new home for now.

I pull up the steep driveway and into a hidden parking lot behind the school. From there, I see another one of our host district's school buildings, busy with children mastering the monkey bars and foursquare. Surrounding both schools are upstate's forested hills, lush with splendor. The city and the countryside dissolve into each other where these two schools sit.

From across the field, little hands leave their monkey bars and wave to the teachers walking in. I see Becky and Mrs. Marion wave back as I choose a parking spot near a large maple tree standing sentinel at the edge of the lot. He is already host to quite a few crows' nests and seems to welcome me and my fellow castaways. It all feels friendly, their large urban district embracing our little rural one.

I follow Mrs. Darling and Mr. Goras through an unmarked door off the parking lot and right into the cafeteria for our first faculty meeting. Despite the gloom of each step, we take in our new surroundings. We look around and even up, as curious as our students will be. We see the ceilings and their familiar pock-marked tiles. On the cinder-block walls, we notice that strange shade of yellowish orange we know from our own elementary edifices, an in-law to the color of our buses. She feels familiar, a cousin of our flooded school and the one I attended as a child. Although she is old, she is ready for us. We are each other's surprising next step.

There is already a clamor in the kitchen as our cook staff sets up shop. Our principal stands at the other end of the room in front of a four-foot-high wooden stage with its big blue curtain drawn behind her. This room is a 1960s amalgamation of cafeteria and auditorium, a place to gather for music and meals. She is framed by old motivational posters, some of their corners coming unfastened from the wall in summer's humidity. They flap in the breeze of a great black fan I've only ever seen the likes of in other schools. Most of the posters are encouraging kids to read, with photos of famous athletes arm in arm with storybook characters who are just as famous.

One particularly flappy poster features Harry Potter and his phoenix with a pile of books under the yellow lightning-bolt words: *Reading Is Magic.* I took great comfort in these stories through my college years, especially after a fire engulfed the entire block of Boston brownstones where I'd been living during my sophomore year. The next semester, I got my first apartment and two kittens. I named the white one Ash, and the orange one Phoenix, and I adopted the motto: *Rise from your cinders.* I think of Ash and Phoenix curled comfortably back home and the message I wanted to send to my future self. *Message received.*

I slide my legs over the benches rooted to their long cafeteria tables, still watching the Phoenix flap in the currents from the fan.

"Welcome to Union West Elementary School," Mrs. Hawkins says. She is strong and grounded, even through the signs of her own sleepless nights.

"Despite the misfortune of the past three days, we are incredibly fortunate that this building is available for us. For those of you who don't know, Union Central had just closed this school in June and consolidated it with the one across campus. It was something they needed to do, but closing a school is always sad. They are all happy to know that children will be learning within these walls again."

A few stragglers sneak in the open door and stand in the back. "Today you'll see a smattering of leftover furniture and equipment the Union Schools were storing here. Their grounds crew will be bringing over any more they can spare this afternoon."

The fourth-grade teachers reach for each other's hands as if we are in church and our prayers have been answered. "Half the gym is set aside for the donations of furniture and school supplies that we are already receiving. There have been outpourings from everywhere. You can go there to begin getting what you need after the tour."

The kindness of these strangers consumes us. I see many teachers quickly dabbing the corners of their eyes, unexpectedly verklempt. I've never needed this sort of help before, and I've never been so grateful. I silently vow to pay this kindness forward for as long as I can.

Mrs. Hawkins leads us around like a kindergarten class on our first day. She takes us to every room, narrating who is assigned to each one. The school seems to welcome us too, thankful that we are filling her emptiness with our need. When the tour is over, classroom teachers disperse to ready their new rooms. Those of us who specialize in small and large groups are left, as those in charge decide where they can put us.

There is a book storage closet that will be the reading teacher's intervention room. The math lab will be in the copy room, which is also serving as both the teachers' lunchroom and additional storage for books and manipulatives. All our special education teachers will be sharing an oversized classroom with partitions for their student interventions. And, finally, when the cafetorium isn't a cafeteria for lunch and breakfast, it will be used for occupational and physical therapy. When it isn't being employed for OT/PT, it will be used for Speech and English as a Second Language interventions. And when it is not being used for any one of those—and sometimes when it is—it will also be the band room.

Since we will all be traveling between schools to do our jobs, I sit down with the ESL, Speech, OT, and PT teachers to create a shared schedule for use of the cafetorium stage. Our mission—there is no "should we choose to accept it"—is to create a schedule that enables us to travel to our other buildings on opposite days and share similar spaces in those schools with other teachers there.

We will all travel to the middle school campus to teach fifth grade. The Speech, OT, and PT teachers also must travel to another, even older school where our universal prekindergarten (UPK) classes are being housed. And of course, most of them were already traveling to our high school and second elementary school. Within a few hours, we have a simple schedule for the stage that accommodates the needs of all thirteen grade levels, all five schools, and the countless other teachers and programs our schedules intersect with. On the outskirts of every school's schedule, we connect them all.

Once we've nailed down the schedule, we head to the gym to pick out some supplies from the leftovers. The middle school principal, Mr. Muskie, has been sent here to monitor and distribute donations. He does a great job of directing traffic and keeping us on our best behavior. I grab pencils, masking tape, and index cards. A solid start. We find a student desk and chair that will serve as our shared teacher station. It fits perfectly under the backstage box for the cafetorium PA's assistive listening equipment.

I fold one of my index cards over on itself to steady the rocking from the desk's uneven legs and secure the corner of the flopping *Harry Potter* poster with a bit of donated masking tape. Our occupational therapist, Mr. Peak, finds a big cabinet and helps me haul it to the stage to hold percussion gear and music we have yet to acquire. Little do we know, it will serve as the elementary school's percussion cabinet for at least the next fifteen years. Backstage, under a maze of hissing pipes, I count thirty-five black stands and sixty chairs of all sorts left by the other school. Behind those I find a tangle of ropes and a square wooden plank.

"Mr. Peak," I say, "do you know what this is?"

"It looks like a sensory swing," he says to himself as I hand the tangled mess to him.

He immediately looks up to find the hook he needs to use it. We smile for the first time at these unexpected gifts, knowing we are occupying the same spaces as our predecessors—making it work, just like they did.

We agree to leave our equipment up against the walls and the main area open for interventions and setups of any kind. My first task upon each arrival will be to set up the chairs and stands for band. My last task will be to strike them. My own high school band director used to say, "Ninety percent furniture mover, ten percent music teacher. Don't like it, don't do it." His words have never been truer, but I find that I like my everlasting workout. Its predictability comforts me, and it comes free of charge. Never needing to pay for a gym membership will always be one of my favorite perks of the job.

As we finish setting up, Mrs. Hawkins arrives. We proudly show her our schedule, but she just nods, already oversaturated with too many details. "If it works, great," she says. Honestly, our schedule looks as crazy and cluttered as our shared space. But we've worked it out, and that's all that matters. We could be in the way, often forgotten about, and left having to cancel our classes when assemblies are scheduled in this already overshared space. But like this hill-hugged nexus of two schools, we are the place where unlikely and even apparently opposing elements combine to change each other.

Back home with my young family and my cats, Ash and Phoenix, I replay the scenes of the day, knowing many others have no homes to go to. Over dinner, I tell my husband and our messy toddler about discovering what would have been an abandoned school if we didn't need it.

For years I've heard our upstate area described as a post-industrial and depressed region. Now, as much as ever, that feels true. But maybe that's how it has to feel when you live on a threshold where things are coming and going. I stroke my little orange and white tabbies, holding them and my son in my lap. I named my furry companions knowing you have to have ashes before you can be reborn from them, but today I find we are really reborn from each other's.

Returning

THERE ARE SO MANY DONATIONS that half the gym can hardly hold them all. Once we all have furniture, Becky and I take trips together to this school supply supermarket to get things as we realize we need them: a stapler, a sharpener, paper clips, rubber bands, something to hold them all. We all remake our rooms with donations from the desks of other benevolent educators.

For weeks after the flood, neighboring community groups host instrument drives for us. One especially active campaign, forty minutes north, is spearheaded by my compassionate and energetic mother-in-law. The music shop there acts as a drop-off point, and they even add a few instruments to the donation pile themselves. Their road rep makes a special trip all the way to us in their delivery van with everything they've collected.

Lonnie stops by with a few instruments from the antique shop. Mr. F brings a few sets of drumsticks and practice pads. Other local music teachers bring instruments, often in pairs like the animals of Noah's Ark. Retired directors stream in steadily with reeds and valve oil—along with stories from their tenures—knowing these essentials will be forgotten if they don't. I accept them all with profound appreciation, writing thank-you cards each night that will never truly convey the depth of my gratitude. I meet the past directors of my current post and many local music teachers for the first time in this hour of need. The instruments they bring are well-worn, replete with quirks and flaws, but we are operational because of their generosity.

School starts, and the bus ride to the new school is so long, many kindergarteners have wet their pants before they even arrive. Many others have gotten sick on themselves going over backroad hills on the way. Compassionate teachers lead these little ones to the nurse for a change of clothes, since they don't know the way. Thankfully, we have loads of volunteers to help with our first day.

Around fifty percent of our students are homeless. Many of them are living with extended family or friends who live up on the hills, away from the village in the Valley. Some come to school with nothing. Volunteers take them to our gym to pick out backpacks and get other essentials. Every adult gives one hundred percent to support them as well as we can.

Mrs. DuBois helps her own blonde-haired daughter off the bus and leads her to her first-grade classroom. They live by the river. I heard Mrs. Ferri saying they lost their entire first floor to the flood.

I am assigned to help lead third graders to their wing of the building. "Third graders, over here," I announce, waving my hand. Julian Finch steps off the bus with his arm around a friend. His sister Lynn is at the middle school with the other fifth graders.

"Come on, Matthew," he says to the boy. "Let's see if we can figure out those intercom codes at this school!"

They know about those, I think to myself. Matthew manages a weak smile, and I see he has nothing with him. I realize Julian is trying to cheer him up. He has a talent for it. James bounds over too, and within minutes Matthew is laughing. The brown-eyed twins, Violet and Valerie, follow close behind James. "Okay, third graders, follow me." I don't line them up, so they follow me in a little pack. The boys chatter about everything they see, while the twins seem to converse telepathically. They are all excited to be on an adventure with each other. Overall, they are far less nervous than I thought they would be. They are built for resilience and each other.

The demolition crew begins to excavate the flooded school site, and items are slowly returned to each teacher, labeled with their room number scribbled in black Sharpie on hastily ripped strips of masking tape. Not much is salvaged. Anything that was stored below four and a half feet has been molding in the moist aftermath and must be thrown away.

As I wait to find out what was recoverable from our band room, I hear that all paper products are being disposed of, destroyed by the high humidity: diplomas, photographs, and of course, the small manila folder I had tucked in my bottom right-hand desk drawer, with the simple scrawl of "Student File" on the outside.

"Make a box and fill it," had been my only assignment. And now I have nothing to show for it. I feel like a failure, and regret surges through me as I think about the box I should have made by now and taken home where it would be safe.

The delivery of the band room's contents is one of the last. It arrives late on a Tuesday afternoon, just as Becky and Mrs. Marion are helping their troop of Girl Scouts don their brown uniforms for their weekly meeting in the cafetorium. Violet and Valerie are wearing identical sashes while a pair of friends, who seem just as close, pull wrinkled vests from their backpacks.

"Ashton, will you help pass out snacks?" Becky asks.

"Can Rose help me? You always say take a buddy everywhere you go when we're camping..."

Becky smiles back at the inseparable pair. "Of course."

I help the crew carry our cases to tables across from the girls, thanking the team as they leave for the day. I should leave too, but I decide to stay and inventory what little has returned to me. I call Dan to tell him I'll be late.

"No problem," he says. "I'll get started making dinner. Take your time." He knows I've been waiting for this.

A few of our oldest instruments, which I had tucked up high because they were of little use, are of course returned. This includes the saxophone whose case I once fixed in Miss Clay's art room. Looking up its serial number online, we eventually determined it was made in 1912. "Great," I mumble as I place its case on the stage. "At least we can give you a one-hundredth birthday party next year."

Of course, Murphy's Law would ensure that I receive back mostly the misfits of my fleet. Protected by their uselessness and irreversible age, these antiques somehow survived the destructive force their youthful counterparts did not. While the work of my most recent years has been washed away, it seems the old is ever enduring. I'd been looking forward to this moment as I saw the contents of other rooms being delivered, but now I find myself fighting off a flash of anger. It feels like such a slap in the face to receive back these useless items.

The truth is, I'm tired. Tired of trying so hard and hiding it from the children that surround me. Tired because the days are long, and nights with a toddler are too.

The Scouts have moved on from their snacking and are

now reciting words I know by heart from my own youth spent in these same meetings. "To help people at all times and to live by the Girl Scout Law," I find myself reciting quietly along with them. Saying the words calms me just enough to continue. I set out what remains of my former crew to attempt a new level of instrument resurrection.

"Okay, guys..." I say to them. "Game for another round?"

I thoroughly sanitize them. Then I play-test each awful instrument, write down what I need to get them working again, and tag the rest for my overworked repair shop. The Scouts move on to a craft associated with their next badge. The cafetorium is alive with their laughter and the interjections of my instrumental diagnostic exams. Still, my mood hasn't lifted much.

I leave the centenarian saxophone for last, knowing already that he is unplayable. Part of me never intends to open his latches. But as I start to set him on the shelf, the Scouts are singing a familiar tune: *"Make new friends, but keep the old..."* And I pause to reconsider.

He has lived through two World Wars and everything in between. He is one of the few connections I have to a place that will live only in my memory from now on. I take him back to the table and open the case. The familiar musk of ancient cat pee and attic greet me along with something else...

"What?" I just stare at it. "How did you get in here?" I say, gently picking up the familiar little clothespin.

Someone on the demolition crew must have seen it and snuck it back to me in the safekeeping of this lowly saxophone case. I wonder how many gifts this emissary of kindness has sent back to the other teachers, or if something struck him about the way this little clothespin just hung on.

"Assignment complete," I whisper to the saxophone. I close the case and click the latches. "Thank you," I say. "You both made it back."

I walk to my desk, tucked behind the curtains of the cafetorium stage with the computer Mr. F found for me, and pin the clothespin to the top of my monitor once more. Which reminds me of something else. I pull up a file on my flash drive titled "If—" and print a new copy of the poem to hang on my wall. I didn't expect holding on to be so hard, but thinking of this new unknown friend and my lovely longtime ones gives me just enough strength to do so.

I place the saxophone on a shelf that's not so high up, and among these messengers from our lost world, I start a new inventory on that old, slow computer. Sadly, the colorfully painted bass drum doesn't make it, nor does the new shiny tuba I drove to the north country to get just weeks ago.

The instruments that did make it keep their old gold numbers and gain new silver ones, tattoos of their membership in both worlds. I stand back to inspect my puny battalion. They take their places beside our donations, all equally signed on for our next adventure. Each one carries its own unseen clothespin, a kernel of anonymous kindness. They are just like us, except that people get tired when we've been treading water for too long.

Even with my clothespin's encouragement, I arrive at lunch the next day flooded with fatigue, needing something akin to Club Fed to energize me. But Becky's schedule doesn't line up with mine, and there is no space for that here, anyway, packed in with books and the constant jamming of our copy machine. I hear the tired teachers try to talk, but too much has changed for us to even know what's causing our troubles. This year, we are all first-year teachers with no veteran perspective to guide us. We've lost so many of the lessons we'd tucked in tidy places and quietly passed from person to person: our clothespins in cases.

I feel like I need a Scout troop of my own, complete with snacks, badges, and most of all, encouragement.

The copy machine jams again.

Everyone sighs, and I wonder how much of our history, our hopes, and ourselves we have lost in twenty-four hours and twelve inches of rain.

The President's Own

EVEN THOUGH WE ARE TIRED, we don't give up. In the months that follow, we slowly remake our program from the continued donations of instruments, music, and the generosity of others. I make many trips to Lonnie's shop, and our booster club continues to help us buy used instruments—our "new" fleet that is not so unlike our original one, assembled from the forgotten treasures of other times. Mr. F lends us supplies, music, and instruments the secondary school can survive without. After my morning lessons with our fifth graders, I pack the back seat of my sedan with these donations and bring them to our elementary school for the beginners. Once again, we somehow get something for everyone who wants to play.

I submit our entire outdated and irrelevant inventory to the school officials, who demand it for insurance purposes. It is immaculate by this point. Last summer before the flood, motivated by some unknown force, I inventoried everything in the room, down to the last drumstick. But it doesn't matter. In the reality of the crisis, we are forgotten.

While we wait for insurance, or FEMA, or the school, or whoever is officially supposed to help us, we open letters from students in other flooded schools. We line our halls with their art depicting children dancing in the rain, and we find the greatest help comes from those who are hurting just like us.

One early morning, I open a manila envelope from the "President's Own Marine Band" at my rickety desk behind the cafetorium curtains. It is beautifully written, printed on the Band's elegant letterhead. They've heard what the flood did to our school and encourage us, always faithful, in our efforts onward. In addition, they've sent a band's worth of Marine Band stickers to adorn our replacement instrument cases.

Alone, in morning's womb of darkness, their confidence washes over me. At our afternoon rehearsal, I read their letter to our band, and my students sit taller hearing the encouragement sent specifically to them—from the President's *Own* Band! Together we brand every donation with the Marine Band's stickers and our uncertain hope. They leave rehearsal, heads high for the first time since the flood, brandishing their new badges for all to see. With this one act of kindness, we've become the President's Own Elementary Band, and the donations finally feel like our own.

I bring the Marine Band's ordinary and now empty manila envelope to my desk. Before the flood, I would have thrown it away, but instead, on its outside, I write "Student File" in my blocky italicized script. To their letter, I add the notes and artwork from the other flooded bands. The envelope that delivered their seeds of hope now holds some of our own. I lay it on the bottom level of a bookshelf I've fashioned from cardboard boxes to hold the sheets of music I type out each night for the next day's lessons.

We never stop feeling like the President's Own. Inspired by them, we write our own letters to other flooded schools. Sometimes the only thing you can do is give others the gift you need to receive most yourself.

The students leave their cases on the edge of the stage, stickers facing out so everyone can see them. They grab them every afternoon on their rush to the bus. They eat, sleep, and practice in the trailers parked in their driveways, and they help their parents demolish the dry wall of their homes during every spare second. Many live without heat in their homes through November. There is no dress code for the winter concert; they come in what they have. Our only uniform is the stickers on our cases.

Some days it feels as though the flood has destroyed everything, and in many ways it has. Mr. O'Dell allows one last staff photo in front of our sunken schoolhouse before they demolish it, and Mrs. Darling makes Christmas ornaments out of the keys that once opened our classroom doors but now lead nowhere.

We never do return to the school we knew, or its perfectly balanced ecosystem. Everyone eventually finds ways of moving on. Some of us rebuild buildings and acquire all manner of new things. Others leave for opportunities elsewhere. Many more stay, but not with the same spirit. There are a few of us, however, whose convictions grow anew. We slowly find each other and band together with silent, unseen threads of dolor and devotedness, which are the building blocks of strength, as we have come to know.

YEAR SIX

"If you can wait and not be tired by waiting,
Or being lied about, don't deal in lies,"

~Rudyard Kipling

The Cafetorium

I BEGIN ANOTHER SCHOOL YEAR, ready to stay in this building for whatever indefinite amount of time it takes to rebuild ours. The cafeteria is still our classroom. The stage can barely house rehearsals, and with my morning sickness for Baby Number Two, I am losing my appetite for lunchtime lessons more every day. I am setting up for our anticipated beginner band demo to the shrieks of second grade socialization and the smells of Taco Tuesday, when I think, *If I ever write a book, I'll call it* Making It Work.

The fourth-grade classes arrive, and I introduce myself, but most of these students already know who I am. I certainly know who they are. I've been watching them grow ever since our first day together with Mrs. Darling, waiting for my pre-K clan to become my fourth-grade band.

I look down at the script I've written for myself and then out at them all. After five years of first days and beginner demos, I understand they are not just deciding which instrument to play. They are deciding on me. I could tell them about my conservatory education and the few accolades I've earned, but I know my audience. Mr. F's words ring in my ears:

They take the teacher, not the class.

So instead, I say, "I'm going to tell you three true statements about myself before we get started. I can play the trumpet standing on my head, I can drive a tractor, and I can't wait to meet each of you in your lessons."

The fourth graders find this funny enough, and so I continue with the demo, introducing each instrument and taking questions as I go. Though I've planned to perform only fourth grade favorites like "SpongeBob" and "Star Wars," when I get to my own instrument—the flute—I find my fingers playing the first few bars of my own favorite, "The Hills Are Alive."

"Does anyone know that tune?" I ask after I cadence. A few hands shoot right up, and one of them is Julian Finch's.

"Oo, oo! I know! I know!" my mini theater maniacs affirm. "It's from *The Sound of Music*."

Engaging this audience is easy. I wade through the woodwinds, hiding the always popular percussion in the middle and leaving the underappreciated low brass for last. My aim is to balance the band with students choosing a variety of instruments, but this can be difficult when working with ten-year-olds who want nothing more than to parallel their peers.

I've hidden a trombone and euphonium under a big navy-blue sheet, talking up the strength and character of the students who play these mystery instruments after demoing each of the others. Finally I reveal them, pulling away the sheet with an excess of showmanship both matadors and magicians would be proud of. I conclude the demonstration with a heartfelt rendition of "Take Me Out to the Ballgame" on the trombone, showing off its glorious capacity for glissandos and plunger mutes.

When we reach the concluding question-and-answer

session, nearly all their hands shoot up. Some have questions. Most just want to tell me their own anecdotes.

"Do you remember my brother?"

"Did ya teach my neighbor?"

"I'm gonna play my mom's clarinet."

"I'm borrowing my cousin's saxophone."

"Can we play harmonica in band? Accordion? Banjo?"

"Are you pregnant?"

"Do you know what it is yet?"

"Yes, I am," I laugh. "And you'll just have to wait and see."

This has got to be the chattiest group I've met yet and I am instantly entertained by them. Excitement seeps from their fidgety bodies as they wait for their forms, imagining their success on shiny new instruments. They don't know our instruments aren't new, or how sweaty success will be, but they supply the spark needed to start this engine. My job as their conductor is just to stoke their kindling into the fire each of their destinations demands.

I hand out interest forms, announcing that school-supplied instruments are assigned on a first come, first served basis, and we often run out of the most popular choices. Nearly everything is the same as demo days in our old building, but I know this is the one I'll remember when I look back upon all the years of doing them.

Dismissal has barely started when parents are barraged with my beginner band permission forms. Papers fly back to me with frenzied children racing to win their first choice. Their excitement is infectious. Never has a piece of paper felt more like one of Wonka's Golden Tickets.

"Did we get it? Did we get the flute?" two little voices plead. I remember them from Mrs. Marion's Scouts session after school. "We need to play the flute!" They push their freshly signed permission papers back into my hands, and I read the two girls' names.

"Don't worry, Rose and..." I shift the papers to confirm the second name. "...Ashton. You'll both know soon," I assure them like the doctor assures me at each of my baby checkups. "I find these things always have a way of working out."

They hurry home, fingers crossed, reciting their twin prayers of "Flute, flute, *please* be flute."

For the next week, I curate the year's roster, finally filling it with the names of the pre-K pupils I met at drop-off on my first day as a teacher—*six years* ago. The brown-eyed twins, Violet and Valerie (who've both signed up for clarinet); the Capuchin Monkey Child, James; and the Final Finch, Julian, are joined by many others, including my flute fanatics, Rose and Ashton. I remember them sitting in the first row at my first winter concert. Time has passed so quickly in a way, and I feel conflicted, with the joy of a new baby taking time away from this group I have been waiting to work with.

They are the first students to know only me as the director here, the memory of the men who came before me now gone. Many have seen their siblings shine in impressive performances of the past, but it will be impossible to recreate those moments for them, displaced as we are. This is not what I had imagined for them, but we start together anyhow, dented instruments in hand, knowing no other way but forward.

I post the first lesson schedule, and thus their first objective: Know your time and be there for it. Once they are ready, the band will rehearse together at the end of the day, all seventy-five of them. But before we can do that, we pull them out of class by group to teach them, in thirty-minute sessions, the specifics of their instruments that are impossible to teach in the big band setting.

It is also our profession's way of creating meaningful connections with each student, since the large band rehearsals can be impersonal and even intimidating by nature. There is simply not enough time to give each of the seventy-five musicians even one piece of tailored feedback in a thirty-minute rehearsal. So we start like this—as our teachers started with us—and section by section, lesson by pull-out lesson, we build our band.

Time-telling on analog clocks is suddenly all too relevant, and students now hone this tricky skill in the seconds before each lesson starts. We're unable to close the doors on our open cafeteria, so the sound of beginner band wafts through the halls of the entire school, punctuated by feet moving faster than they should at precise half-hour intervals down the fourth-grade hallway.

In the beginning, I pull the dusty curtain closed during the clamorous lunch periods, but it is still too loud to teach or tell them anything at all. So I contact a classroom teacher from each grade level and ask if I can teach lessons in their room during their grade's lunch. Every teacher says yes, even though it's their only time for peace and quiet all day. I try to rotate rooms when possible to avoid out-staying our welcome in any one place, but not a single teacher complains.

I attach an old milk crate with some bungee cords to a small, abandoned dolly, load it up with folding stands, lesson books, pencils, a little whiteboard, and flash cards, and away we go. I meet each lesson group by the stage's side door and leave a note there on another whiteboard indicating which classroom we have gone to. Our bandwagon then adventures to each wing of the school, cases swinging playfully at their sides.

"Where we going today?" Julian Finch asks as James slides down the railing of the stage stairs, drumsticks in hand. Before

I can answer, their French horn compatriot Matthew observes, "Kindergarteners are eating lunch, so I bet we'll be going to one of their classrooms."

"Very astute," I say as we set off down the hall.

Since they didn't attend the lower grades here, these trips to unknown rooms are an interesting change of pace for them. Once we arrive, the Three Musketeers put their instruments together while I set up the kindergarten chairs and assemble folding stands. We never get as much done in these lessons due to our travel time, but it is much better than staying on the stage. Today, this classroom's teacher returns early from lunch to finish some work, and the band boys greet her like a long-lost family member.

"Mrs. Myers!" they cry in unison upon her arrival.

She is attacked with hugs from her former students, and I know whatever inconvenience we have caused her has been immediately forgiven by their enduring adoration. After their brief reunion we return to our work as best we can, but my students' eyes wander around the world she has created. It's hard to keep them focused, surrounded by the colorful alphabet posters and number lines of the primary grades.

All fall, amidst the hassle of a carted class and the distraction of my bandsmen, we visit each grade level, and I see for myself that every place has its purpose: each level of learning so essential; each teacher so influential. The students change as they enter their past pedagogues' rooms.

Their gaits and expressions shift as they remember parts of themselves they'd almost forgotten. These teachers have taught their students something intangible and enduring, and I see the teachers change too, as memories return with their pupils. I realize we send little bits of ourselves out into the world with every student we instruct. We can't help it. We try to teach our tidy topics, but we always teach who we are.

At the end of the first marking period, I decide to offer the band members with these lunchtime lessons a chance to stay on the stage. "Instead of going to the classrooms today," I ask them, "how would you like to give a little performance in the cafeteria?" They all think it's a great idea, so for the last lessons before my maternity leave, we open the curtain and play for whichever grade is eating, transforming the cafeteria into a cool café with our own elementary open mic.

The musicians love this, and so do our unsuspecting audiences. Rose and Ashton come down during their recesses, and the soundtrack of my prep period becomes their flute duet rising over the din of second grade lunch. Instead of being in each other's way, we are at the heart of the school, bringing back everything we've learned in those classrooms to the cafetorium's center. Holiday tunes add cheer to the meal before Thanksgiving break, and "We Will Rock You"—the best four note song that ever lived—sends an army of kindergarteners stomping off to conquer their ABC's. Every day is a demo day now.

With our music, we meet the entire school. The students think the whole thing is fabulous, and the lunch ladies seem at least mildly entertained by our on-stage escapades. I certainly don't have the perfect schedule, the perfect room, or the perfectly timed maternity leave, but I'm making it work with the class I've been waiting for. Even if this beginning feels far too fragile, I'm glad we've opened the curtain and begun.

The Perfect Match

HE SITS THERE ON THE STAGE, holding the wrong instrument. I know it immediately after returning from maternity leave, but school is not about what teachers know. It isn't that Julian Finch is particularly suited to something else as some students are, their demeanor and physical attributes matching them with one instrument and no other. He could play anything. He doesn't struggle as he sits in the section of unending trumpet players, eager already to best each other in battles of *better, faster, louder* and—of course, the blockbuster of all brass aptitude—the ever evasive *higher*.

He and his friends settle across the sections of the band, Matthew on trumpet and James—of course—on percussion. Their winter concert brings the novice glory that only the first five notes of concert Bb can provide. But as January "Jingle Bells" rings across the cafetorium, he finally hears what I hear, a band without a bottom, and the silence of those missing voices.

He approaches me after the concert. "I hear you need low brass."

I nod in affirmation, careful not to telegraph my

predictions of his path.

"Then I'll learn trombone for the next concert."

The need was mine, but the choice was his. And just like that, we begin again, in earnest this time. I send the Final Finch home with his newly issued trombone, and he returns the next day knowing everything his older brother Arthur could teach him in one night. Barely off the bus, he schedules a lunchtime lesson to show me, and I'm surprised to find myself looking forward to it all morning.

After his abbreviated meal of a peanut butter bagel sandwich, he jumps on the stage and opens his case, just as he's seen his older brother do so many times. I notice how similar their hands are as he works the slightly-loose-from-overuse latches of his recently donated King 606.

"I've learned my concert B-flat scale," he announces and proceeds to play it for me.

Perfectly.

I try to hide my smile, but I feel a sweet exhilaration rise in my chest. I am present for the beginning of something rare and wonderful. A perfect match.

"What do you think?" I ask, expecting him to tell me if he likes trombone as well as the trumpet.

"Well, the fourth scale degree was a little flat," he replies, testing a few variations of third position.

He is so engrossed in examining his E-flat that he doesn't notice my surprise, or that I am setting a new trajectory for his lessons. This one is close to the music.

"Would you like to try it again?" I ask.

He answers with another set of fifteen neatly placed pitches, metered with a musicianship beyond his years.

"Do you feel better about that one?" I ask.

"The pitch was better," he replies. but I can see there are other things he's heard that he would like to address. He's an artist already, forever existing in that painful place between real and ideal. But he doesn't stall the lesson there. I see him make a mental note for future practice sessions and turn his attention to me once more.

I select a dog-eared *Trombone Book 1* from our stack of donated sheet music at the side of the stage and open it to the first page. I place one of my favorite black Ticonderoga No. 2 pencils on his stand and dial a metronome to sixty beats per minute. Then we begin.

I take him through every step intentionally, being careful to skip nothing, even if he appears not to need it. He watches me intently, serious for one so young. I conclude the session with instructions on practice methods and encourage him to work through the book methodically.

"When you go home tonight, relive the lesson," I say, experimenting with these newly adopted words from Mr. F. Our worlds intersect daily at the other school, where I instruct the fifth graders. Every time I overhear him teach, I collect some priceless phrase and wonder if he's spoken more for his students or me to hear. I ferry these gems back with me, along with techniques gleaned from Frank Battisti's books. Then I secretly try them on in each lesson, purposefully seeing which ones fit and which ones will remain theirs.

"I promise not to hold you to some prescribed pace," I continue, "if you promise not to rush through what appears easy. The slower you practice, the faster you learn." These words are also not mine, but the promise is. They are a mantra from my own middle school band director, and their importance grows with each student I pass them to. This is my tribute and connection to the teachers who mattered most to me.

"Deal," he agrees and offers me his hand.

We shake on it, and he feels like my equal. He is nine; I am twenty-eight. But artists are ageless. We meet each other in music, where time means something else, and from then on I never talk to him as if he's nine.

Because he's not. Not really.

We repeat a few of these sessions, and I soon reunite him with his comrades, James and Matthew. Most lessons are grouped by section, coming in cute groups of identical flutes or matching consorts of saxophones. Amidst the many lessons of look-alikes, these Three Musketeers are an odd combination of valves, slides, and drumsticks. And yet, they make their own sense.

They've all already had previous instruction on other instruments, and so they move fluently through reading music. I lump them together because my schedule does not allow me to teach them separately and I see something similar in them that eclipses their disparate instruments, something rare and wonderful. Another perfect match.

It takes extra time to explain new techniques in three ways, but they are interested to hear how the other instruments work and enjoy knowing the challenges their friends face.

"I'm sorry," I say after one lengthy explanation of the vastly different techniques involved in producing a simple slur on xylophone, trombone, and French horn.

"Ehh," shrugs James. "It's cool to know things."

He teaches me in five words that time is never wasted with friends. And so they learn to appreciate each other from the beginning in their unconventional collective.

James began his private drum lessons with Mr. F in third grade and he already stands behind his drum with the same assuredness as his teacher. There is nothing I can teach him Mr. F can't, so I strike another deal with him.

"Since you are getting such excellent instruction already, how about we only play mallet percussion in our lessons here? Snare with Mr. F, mallets with me, and I promise you'll play a little bit of everything in the band, so you won't be bored."

I stick out my hand, just like Julian taught me.

"Deal," he says, and we shake on it.

Matthew's arrangement is straightforward and simple. All he wants to do is play French horn. Since he can already read music, he gets a head start and the opportunity to play it two years earlier than usual. I promise he won't have to wait it out on trumpet until some arbitrary age and switch him the next week. He is happy, and so am I. Another deal.

Their deal with each other has a different currency: friendly competition. They take their lessons standing, proving their skill more to each other than to me. They spur one another on, perfecting scales, sight reading, and solos to perform for adjudicators at our yearly New York State School Music Association (NYSSMA®) festivals.

Years later, I won't remember their scores, but I'll remember our work. I'll remember meeting them outside the adjudicator's door after their performances. I'll remember their flushed faces and their play-by-play recounts of events I'd just witnessed with their parents, through slats in the big brown doors, at the same festival site I attended in my youth. I'll remember their breathless elation as they pack up their instruments with a newfound discovery of their own abilities. Most of all, I'll remember the way they greeted each other, in success or otherwise, with their secret handshakes and the solidarity of their kindred spirits.

In their own way, each lesson group is like this. Rose and Ashton—my "flute-loops," as I fondly call them—grow into vivacious masters of their metronomes, aligning their lives with each other's, one click at a time. They are completely unaware of the inequity of their flooded situation. They do not know what they do not have.

Instead, they are focused on the friends around them. The twins, Violet and Valerie, quietly smile over their clarinets as saxophonists duel with jaunty duets of "Careless Whispers" and "Baby Shark." From the back row, legions of low brass blast ceaseless renditions of "Seven Nation Army" to each other in every available second between opening their cases and the start of class. Their excitement is unabashed, uncontainable, and without a doubt, contagious.

As spring returns, we seize opportunities only available to the displaced. When we walk across the clover and crabgrass field for a band exchange with our host school district, we see pairs of stand partners just like our own, who have found in each other someone who will always turn their page or put their folder back when they are having a bad day.

I meet their director with a sturdy handshake, and the exchange begins. We play similar pieces for each other, sharing the universal enthusiasm our music world holds for "Star Wars." We make sure, of course, to substitute our usual batons for light sabers. Objectively, both our bands lack many of the things I once believed essential for a strong program: nice instruments, new music, a stable schedule, lots of funding. But in missing those things, these students have gained others in spades—life experience, gratitude, and spunk.

You can hear it when they play.

Following my band back across the crabgrass, I see many stand partners sticking side by side just like my brown-eyed twins. Trumpeters' arms hang over each other's shoulders. Percussionists walk perfectly in step. Adoring flute fingers intertwine with one another. And the Three Musketeers are inseparable as always. They've found lifelong friends behind the black stands of our band, and I've found what I feared the flood had extinguished for me in each one of them.

As the band slips by, two-by-two through the side door, I see my flutists' fingers break apart in front of me. A delicate hand reaches down and plucks from the crabgrass a dainty four-leaf clover. Everyone else has walked right by it, but this one saw something special right in front of her.

Without hesitation, Rose hands it to Ashton by her side.

"I find them everywhere," she whispers. "This one's yours."

"I want to find something special to give to you too!" Ashton answers.

"But you already have," Rose says simply.

And from the back of the pack, I again see something rare and wonderful: a deal that sweetens the path before them and hands to help every step of the way. A perfect match.

"We are lucky!" Ashton replies, flinging her arms around Rose in an enormous hug.

Yes, we are, I think, finally allowing myself to feel it too. Yes, we are.

Sisyphus

Journal Entry
June 2013

To All My Students,

The thing I hate the most is saying goodbye. Every year we, your teachers, throw ourselves into school with all our hearts, knowing this is the only 4th grade year you will ever get, and this is our only chance to make yours a good one. We work hard, and for a year— in our lucky case two years—we spend nearly every day together. For this short time, we are the world to each other. We steadily improve, and at the end of next year, right when I feel the real work beginning, I'll let you go, like all the others. I'll watch you sail through that glorious summer vacation to your next grade level, in that far off middle school, while I use summer to prepare your abandoned instruments for the next bunch. Back to the bottom to push this boulder of beginners up the hill of "Hot Cross Buns."

From the outside, it may seem like some strange form of torture, that a person who loves beautiful music so much should be subjected to the relentless auditory assault of these same 3 pitches—9 lessons a day, 5 days a week, for years on end. My conservative estimate of how many times I've heard "Hot Cross Buns" is 45,360, yet still my heart breaks with every class that leaves.

This feeling is part of what made me want my own children. It makes me appreciate every day together. It also moves me forward. It makes me wish there was a way to see any and all of you through your next step, even though it's all out of my comfort zone. I imagine it's better than the heartbreak.

Maybe that's why we fall on tradition. So that every time we hear those tunes, we remember each of you. We remember every student who has ever walked through these doors and tried. These three notes connect each separate class, weaving a tapestry of collective experience and memory, in a band that spans ages and crosses the boundaries of time. In this trio of pitches, you are here, no matter how long you've been gone. Perhaps we parents and teachers tire of hearing these same weary, worn-out tunes. But for you, this year, it's all brand new. Whether it is the 1st time or the 45,361st time, we share what would have otherwise been a solitary struggle, one note at a time.

Always,

Your teacher

Year Seven

"Or being hated, don't give way to hating,
And yet don't look too good, nor talk too wise:"

~Rudyard Kipling

Dreams & Doors

IN SUMMER, SCHOOL DOESN'T GET IN THE WAY of our studies. There is time to teach without urgency, time to learn what we need and miss most during the year. In summer's warm incubator, everyone dreams. Children build tree houses, pillow forts, and sandcastles; teachers reflect on the past year, and whether they want another year like it. In the summer, new teachers arrive and others leave, and all of us wonder what opportunities the new school year will bring.

The shared middle and high-school music wing is my summer lesson space. On my way to it, I pass the fireman statue and the site of our old elementary school. The construction crews are raising the new building and reshaping the earth around it to mitigate future floods. I taught one class here my first year too—although it was only a temporary assignment—and with my old elementary school gone, this is the only school that holds any history for me now. In August, I teach a few afternoon lessons and prepare for another year— alongside Mr. F. once again, albeit now with a little more experience of my own.

In these familiar half-lit halls of summer, I see her the same way Becky first saw me: Our new middle school chorus teacher is getting her welcome tour from the principal, Mr. Muskie. At the sound of their voices, Mr. F emerges from his band room door and welcomes them the way I imagine Santa Claus might invite new elves to his frigid workshop. This whole place is his, and he loves it. He's had a hand in the creation of every inch of it: each room, course, and concert tradition. With the latest retirement, he is now the maven of our department, I am no longer the newbie, and our matriarch, Mrs. Doyen, is moving on.

After thirty-eight years, she has more experience teaching than I do living. I am curious about all the reasons she stayed for so long, and all the reasons she is leaving now. I asked her last year how she knew it was time to move on, and she said, "I just know. And when it's time for you, you'll know just like I do."

I wonder: *Will I make it to year thirty-eight? Is that even my goal?* I don't know the answer.

I've been so focused on objectives for my students that I've forgotten my own. There has been no scaffolded curriculum to take me from year one to year thirty. In fact, most of the teachers hired with me are already gone, and I have to wonder, how many "Hot Cross Buns" will it take to earn Mrs. Doyen's brand of wisdom?

Mr. Muskie introduces us to the new chorus teacher, Miss Garnet, and she sweeps her long blond hair (tipped in pink) over her shoulder as she reaches for our first handshake— genuine, just like her.

"Nice to meet you," she says with an energy I've missed since Miss Clay moved away. Miss Garnet follows Mr. Muskie past an open door to an abandoned courtyard and into her new room farther down the hall.

"We are lucky to get her so late in August," Mr. F says to

me. "Hopefully, we can keep her. She's a good one."

"Who's a good one?" Julian chimes in, sticking his head through the courtyard's open door.

"That's me. I'm the good one," James pipes in behind him. "Get used to it."

"What are you doing out there?" I ask.

"Just...exploring," Julian says with a sidelong glance at James, who tucks an old soccer ball covered in yellow pollen under his arm.

I look through the open door to see the grounds crew at the far end of the courtyard running their weed whackers across knee-high goldenrod and pokeweed. I raise my eyebrows at the boys.

"Okay, so we were playing off-road soccer," James admits, dusting the remains of the goldenrod from his soccer ball.

Julian sneezes, and we all laugh. I can see how fond Mr. F has become of James. We return to our rooms for their lessons—James with Mr. F, Julian with me. August wanes gently as Julian perfects his blues scales and James learns to emulate Mr. F's eleven-stroke rolls and dry sense of humor.

Summer evenings and weekends are even more wonderful, full as they are of family. Dan's brother also has a new baby. His son AJ is about the same age as our daughter Saoirse. We get the families together at every opportunity, grilling hot dogs and hamburgers until summer's sunlight gives way to the firsts of another fall. I hold both babies on my lap while Rhyse runs around the yard after a soccer ball with Dan and I. And I think, *There has never been a sweeter summer than this.*

In a normal year, I would be teaching my fifth graders at our elementary school, but since we are still displaced by the flood,

I teach them at the secondary school. Three schools and seven first days later, my original pre-K's look little once again, flung in next to high school seniors, but my students and I are more excited than intimidated.

Julian, James, and Matthew never miss a lesson. They hear the middle schoolers next door and the high schoolers down the hall, and they are eager to play as well as them. One day, after an especially productive lesson, my Musketeers pack up early to beat the lunch line rush. In the hall we hear the high school band rehearsal ending. Trumpets and flutes wail in the stratosphere, while the percussion drives the bass voices home. It's the impressive sound of an ensemble, with every member contributing their best.

"Whoa!" Matthew's jaw drops along with Julian's. "Did you hear that?"

"I certainly did," I say, impressed as well. Their sounds breathe life into the rutted pathways beginner band's B-flat major has gnawed into the gray matter of my brain.

"That's Jeremiah on trumpet," James says. "He practiced that lick all last night."

When the bell rings, Jeremiah strides down the hall with Arthur and Zach, from my very first jazz band. I see all the skills they've gained since leaving me. I see the respect they have for their middle school director, Mr. Bishop, who taught them for a year longer than I did. And I sense their even stronger connection with Mr. F, who gets them for four years, twice as long as me. Although I know it's not only a matter of time, time certainly matters, and I find myself longing again for more of it with the students I have now.

One December day while warming my peppermint tea in the band room microwave, I overhear a sixth-grade percussion lesson. Mr. Bishop is struggling to increase the speed of their paradiddles, so he stops the lesson and remediates their basic sticking pattern with three kinds of strokes: down, up, and tap. I've known about the alternating and double stickings involved from the elementary group's lesson books, but these strokes he's teaching them now are new to me.

I brew my tea a bit longer than needed so I can watch the lesson progress, but I've already learned an important lesson about what I don't know. This is not feedback administrators—musically inclined or not—could have fed me in formal observations. I drink a lot more tea that year and discover what my students have truly learned from me by their success in Mr. Bishop's classes.

Meanwhile, I continue to befriend our new choral teacher, Miss Garnet. Just like Mr. F said, she's a good one, and I hope we can keep her. Remembering my own first year, I offer to help with whatever she needs, hoping I can share a bit of the kindness Miss Clay shared with me.

Together we file music and set tidy arcs of chairs. While we work, we chat about the banal details of surviving on the other side of school's looking glass and gradually we talk of more meaningful matters: staying inspired amidst the insipid, compartmentalizing of how much you care, and—perhaps most importantly—retaining the ability to laugh at the absurdity of it all.

The amount of work is overwhelming for her, just as it was—still is—for me. One daily forty-five-minute prep is not enough to plan for eight classes, enter attendance, manage music, move setups, print concert programs, plan trips, organize fundraisers, balance accounts, curate orders, answer emails, enter grades, update curriculum, collaborate with colleagues, analyze assessment data, call home, write referrals, check the mailbox, and hopefully visit the bathroom.

Searching for something special to give my displaced fifth graders, I commission a piece for their spring concert. Inevitably, some sections prove too difficult for us, and at lunch one day I finally express my misgivings to the other directors. "We're not getting the middle section, and the composer is coming in a month for the concert."

Without missing a bite, Mr. Bishop says, "Why don't you come to the seventh and eighth-grade rehearsal tomorrow. Tell the band about the project and ask for some volunteers to play. I'll give any student who signs up extra credit."

"Same for the high schoolers," adds Mr. F.

"Thank you so much," I say, surprised at the ease with which they found an answer for me.

The next morning, I make my announcement to the middle schoolers, and to my complete surprise a sizable group, led by Lynn Finch and her friends, signs up. I make a similar plea to the high school band, and Anne, Zach, Jeremiah, and Arthur drag their friends along with them to help bolster their kid brothers' band.

I write them passes for activity period. My heart pounds before rehearsal like it's my first one, but I can't turn back now. The composer is coming all the way from Boston, and we must make this work. They arrive excited, and we dig right in. I am terrified I'll have nothing to say, but as soon as I hear their music, I relax. Coaching them now doesn't feel much different than it did when they were fifth graders.

At the dress rehearsal, my fifth graders are bouncing with excitement to play alongside the high schoolers. At one point, I see Arthur lean over and silently show Julian an alternate slide position, while Anne and Lynn lead Rose and Ashton like pied pipers through a series of trills.

That night, we present our performance on the enormous secondary stage. Zach and Jeremiah flank my fifth-grade trumpets, and across the band I see students from all the grades I've taught. I take photos of the group to add to my manila student file back at the elementary school. It's the first time I have worked with older students, and I love it.

So when Mr. Bishop unexpectedly announces his resignation, and therefore the availability of the middle school position, I ask to officially observe his and Mr. F's rehearsal. I watch from the back of the room, trying to picture myself on their podiums. I ask Mr. F questions with a newfound purpose. His advice means so much more to me now that I've seen his skills at work. With Mr. Bishop out for the day, attending to the details of his move, Mr. F runs a middle school rehearsal, while I look on. The bell rings, and in ninety seconds the room is empty of everyone except us. In this unexpected moment, by the band room door, I ask him the question I've been asking myself all year.

"So, do you think I could do it?" He raises his eyebrows above his glasses in question to my cryptic inquiry, so I proceed. "You know, the middle school job. Do you think I could do it?"

I wait a beat before adding tentatively, "Should I?"

It's not until these pent-up words are ringing between us that I realize how much I want this. I've been testing these waters all year. I know I want it because of how impossible it seems—that this once painfully shy and quiet kid could stand in front of these big bands and have something worthwhile enough to say that maniacal middle schoolers might actually listen.

Most of all, I realize I'm asking for his blessing. This is his department. He has watched so many others come and go, off to other dreams while he has built the bands I see before me. The students rise to his standard from an early age because they know they will one day be in *Mr. F's band*. Everyone in our community knows his name from decades of Memorial Day parades and Rotary Club luncheons. We all know he has made a name for himself—and for us— through his work, and I know how much this place means to him.

He hides it well, but I also know he will miss his band buddy. They look forward to every lunch, and whether they are sharing an anecdote or a slice of pie, it's always been more than that. They even look alike. They cross their arms the same way and lean back in the same stance as they wait for the next crew of kids by the band room doors, debriefing from the day's rehearsals. My fifth graders can't even tell them apart. They think the one amazing Mr. F does it all. These two are a dynamic duo, and every one of us feels it. Their partnership goes beyond the bounds of band. Another perfect match.

I know I can never replace what he's losing, and I fear I will only let him down. But just the same—somehow—I have asked him my dubious question. He looks at me through his glasses and my inexperience and states matter-of-factly, "You can."

I want him to tell me more. I want to know what he thinks I should do, but the band room door bangs open with Rose, Ashton, and our next set of customers. I'll have to be content with the advice I've been given. His belief is blessing enough.

"Well," I say, "looks like I've got to go."

"I know," Mr. F replies, opening the band room door for me. "Now go do it."

Rose, Ashton, and I walk next door to our little lesson room, and as Mr. F turns back toward his own, I sense the surprise and satisfaction he tries to hide. I will never know if I saw him smile or if I have just imagined it in the years that have passed since. But I do know Mr. F opened a door for me and encouraged me just enough to walk through it.

Follow Them

"So...WHEN DO YOU FEEL LIKE YOU REALLY STARTED NAILING IT?"

It's late May, and we've been driving for ten minutes with the window down when I ask the question. I'm holding my hair back from the road wind that throws it repeatedly into my face.

"You know, as a teacher?" I prod once he's rolled up the window.

Mr. F looks forward, giving no signal that the conversation has abruptly shifted from small talk to something more personal. He leaves just enough time to think, but not enough for me to question his answer.

"It takes ten years."

The road rumbles as we consider the meaning of this for each of us.

"I've been teaching for seven." I say it just as much to myself as to him. He considers this for a moment.

"I know," he replies. "I've always taught high school, except for my first year here. That year I taught sixth grade and learned the ropes, while the previous high school director prepared for us to switch positions." He glances at me. "That was always the plan."

I contemplate his words over the rollercoaster backroads we drive to interview candidates for the open elementary position I'm vacating. I want to believe he's just encouraging me in my newly made decision to move to middle school. I don't want to notice the gray at the edges of his receding hairline. So I box up any premonitions of a world without him in the driver's seat, and whether I want to or not, I find my fingers nervously twirling one of my curls, a childhood habit I cling to for comfort when the inevitable unsettles me.

"My first year," he says, "I spent the entire summer going through the band room, one box at a time." He breathes with the weight of remembered work. "It took all summer."

I think of my first day discovering the treasures of my now shipwrecked room and realize I'll have to do this all again too. I heard someone say once, "Writers live twice," and recently I've experienced how parents do too, as my family shares every holiday and milestone with my two small children and nephew. But the teacher's secret is that we live again and again, refining the best response for each event in our students' development. When our efforts unavoidably falter the first time, we get to try again and differently next class, next week, next year...until we finally figure it out.

"I always had a special connection with those sixth graders," he says as we close the doors to his big blue van and enter our elementary school. "Their senior year stands out to me even now. It was special."

Special. His story resonates with me as I walk toward the conference room. I know these students I will now move on with are special too. That they will be present for all my first failures in this new job is simultaneously terrifying and motivating. A new thought strikes me: My somewhat selfish move to stay with them cannot be the reason they do not learn life's next lessons. *I cannot be that reason.* I wish I could teach them years from now, when I finally know what I'm doing. The best I can do is promise myself that their senior year will be special too.

So as I sit down across from our first candidate, I decide we will work diligently at every detail. I will accept no excuses from myself or anyone else about budgets, attitudes, or anything at all. Besides, if I ever feel like blaming the teacher who sent them to me, the only person I can blame will be myself. So I vow to take responsibility, to manifest my positivity over every possible thing I can. I will not let them down. I will not let *him* down.

The candidates fidget in their chairs, unsure of what to do with their hands, which they seem to have just noticed they have no good place for. Most of them are young, enthusiastic, and of course, awkward. However, Mr. Bishop's spring student teacher, Mr. Heart, is the winner of the day and the job because of his calm confidence...and because he is the only one to correctly teach a five-stroke roll in the trial lesson. He knows his stuff.

"Another good one," Mr. F affirms on our way out of the interviews. I think of the day's candidates, and I know my next steps will be awkward like theirs as I leave the nest that has nurtured me. I consider all that Mr. Heart is going to have to leave behind to take on this new role as teacher, and I wonder if I've let go of the right things to grow into my own new position.

The Day of Caring is almost here.

Each June our school takes a day to donate our time, services, skills, and talents to make the world nicer for someone else. We do it in honor of the young girl who saved the life of one of our staff members through organ donation. Encouraged by the day, and to signal a shift I sense in myself, I sign up to donate my lengthy curls to a children's cancer charity. Of course, I need an excuse to involve my band members. So I tell them that if we collect enough donations in the school council's food drive (which I know they'll do), I'll donate my hair on the Day of Caring. too.

When the day arrives, one of our wonderful teacher's aides cuts my hair alongside elementary school students who are donating theirs as well. Like flowers from our gardens, we've grown this hair to give it away. We take before-and-after pictures, and everyone smiles at our short new styles. I leave the chair with eleven inches less. It feels good, the breeze on the back of my neck and the weight of my hair off my shoulders.

After the buses leave for summer, I stand on the cafetorium stage one last time. I look at the shelves of donations I've tidied for someone else. I never stopped fixing them. I'd been to Lonnie's shop just last month to get a flute for a student who moved into the district late in the year. I think of the Girl Scouts who met here, and I know that, even with all the upheaval, I have left this place better than when I came. If there was a Scout badge for Beginner Band Instructor, I know I have earned it.

I take one last look and, along with my locks, I let go of the boulder I've been bearing. I give away what I've grown so the next "good one"—Mr. Heart—might grow something of his own. Then I step into summer with my own dreams, taking with me only a clothespin, a poem, and a manila envelope of memories. When I finally take the wheel, I roll the windows all the way down and drive the whole way home with the wind in my face and its breeze on the back of my neck.

Scherzo
Years 8 – 13

"Every Who down in Whoville, the tall and the small,
was singing! Without any presents at all!"

From *How the Grinch Stole Christmas*
by Dr. Seuss

YEAR EIGHT

"If you can dream—and not make dreams your master;
If you can think—and not make thoughts your aim;"

~Rudyard Kipling

Missing Pieces

I SPEND SUMMER GOING THROUGH EVERY BOX in the middle school band room, in part because I should, but more because Mr. F said he did. I inventory every cupboard, discovering Mr. Bishop's tidy rows of neatly labeled Tupperware with supplies for every instrument and occasion. In addition to the essentials, he's left ladders and power tools for set builds, vases for concert flowers, and a humble set of dishes, complete with several pie servers.

His handwriting is everywhere. The instrument cases bear serial numbers stamped in his hand. Boxes of band music display the names of old soloists, and the dates of previous performances are penned neatly in his same trig script. He's left the space ready for me, but he's also stripped the room's walls of his photos and prized pirate posters, giving them to the students who would miss him the most. They left last year with these tokens in their hands, hoping for any way to hold on to him.

My family and I arrive at my next work session with my own adornments, filling the empty spaces where pirate posters once hung with photos of my cats and encouraging words. I tape a copy of "If—" above my computer, where I've already clipped my clothespin. I stash my manila student file folder in the bottom right-hand drawer of my desk. Then I tag pristine instruments with new names, while my children scribble scenes on the whiteboard and dance in the wide-open opportunity an empty band room offers. We work all afternoon, but when I stand back in this outfitted new space, I still feel something is missing....

Fall arrives with my increased enthusiasm riding on my mentor's words: "It takes ten years." I'm almost there. I hope that soon this will feel more natural, easier even. A long line of yellow buses brings the secondary students and my sixth graders to school, past the nearly completed elementary building. I know they feel left out when they see it and when we stand outside to clap for the buses that bring the current elementary students to their first day there. Many of the middle schoolers lost their old school and never received the satisfaction of attending this new one. I know how they feel. We had to move on, whether we wanted to or not.

My sixth graders are sweet, but so much more squirrelly than last year, asking to switch instruments every time I turn around. Still, I love being with them, antics and all. It's time I never thought we would share. Another district elementary school from across the river funnels into our middle school, and their band students join my former pre-K pack, doubling the size and energy of our band along with the challenge to my classroom management skills. I try to recreate the regimented world of my predecessor, but it is much harder than he made it look.

With increasing enrollment, we run out of low-brass instruments, and again my family and I make the trek to

Lonnie's unique antique shop so every student has something to play. He goes off to dig in his storage closet while we walk around the shop with the kids. Rhyse and Saoirse find some old toy cars and run them over the rug while Dan inspects vintage hand tools. I meander past retro water glasses painted with *Looney Tunes* characters, and then...a collection of cigar boxes. I pause when I see them.

Make a box and fill it. Maybe I should pick one up and finally retire my manila folder. There are few that would do. I am still debating when Lonnie returns with his arms full of trombones and a euphonium case dangling at his side. We open the cases, and after my inspection we agree to take the lot. I check out with the kids while Dan packs up the car. It is only on my way home, after the excitement has worn off, that I realize I have forgotten about the box.

Every day I come to school with plans worth paying attention to and new techniques I've read about in Mr. Battisti's books. Teaching D-flat and dotted quarter notes is an absolute rush after seven years of hearing music without either.

After our first concert, my Three Musketeers rally new friends and beg for a sixth-grade jazz band. I can't refuse their contagious enthusiasm, so I offer a weekly lunchtime rehearsal. They are even wilder at this time of day, and although we don't make much musical progress—and I clean up a lot of Twinkie wrappers—we begin to become something more than a band alongside our sandwiches.

My biggest challenge is certainly not the sixth graders. The habits planted by Mr. Bishop are still strong in his seventh and eighth-grade protégés, and I can't be sure if my successes with them are because I'm doing the right thing or because he did.

I fear it's the latter. Our first rehearsals are effective, but as stark and sterile as the white walls around us. I am not their beloved band director, and many students take this out on me with cold demeanors and cutting words. After their concerts I'm left erasing all manner of inappropriate art and editorial addendums from the empty spaces on their original copies of the music. No matter what I put on the walls, the room is not welcoming when they are in it.

I leave rehearsals feeling drained and defeated. Nothing from my band books seems to solve my problems. I work through my lunches and every space in my schedule, searching for the missing piece. Then one day in late December, with our half-hearted winter concerts wrapped up, Mr. F unexpectedly enters the room, interrupting this fruitless hunt with a homemade pie in hand.

"It's time for pie," he announces to the room—even though I am the only one in it.

I look up from my computer. He's humming "Sleigh Ride," which the high school band played for their holiday concert last week.

"Pie?"

"Pie is my favorite food, and it's my birthday. So yes, pie."

Mr. F's every move is intentional, I've learned. He wastes nothing, least of all time—and now, it seems, pie. With him everything is important, so I stop mid-task and follow his lead. He opens one of the cupboards I dissected last summer and selects his favorite server as I move to the table where he and Mr. Bishop shared countless meals. We load up our plates and enjoy the taste of birthday pie.

"Homemade blueberry-peach," he says after the first bite. "My favorite."

I nod, mouth full. I have to admit, it's incredible.

"I've always found that pie can solve problems you can't

quite put your finger on," he says once we've finished. I secretly want seconds, but we save the rest, tucking it in the fridge.

The next day he arrives at the same time, and I release my work to attend to pie leftovers with him. We talk about our favorite pieces and spring program plans, and when the bell rings I feel better. Whatever he's doing, it's helping. It is not the boisterous potluck from my first school, but it means just as much. Maybe more. The third day, he brings salad and stories of "Sleigh Ride" slapstick fiascos to fill the lunch hour.

As I take the empty tin to the trash, I find my Musketeers along with Ashton and Rose, waving at the door with Christmas cards in hand. I welcome them in, and they look suspiciously at the empty tin.

"Have you been eating pie?" Matthew asks incredulously.

Mr. F laughs his big belly laugh.

"Why yes," I answer in our defense. "Is that allowable?"

"Only if you share it with us!" Julian and James exclaim in the sugar-induced excitement of the day before break.

"If you're making another, Ashton likes apple," Rose says with an exaggerated wink.

I look to Mr. F as if he has planted these pie propagandists on purpose.

He looks at them while he says to me, "Apparently you have some smart students." I shrug my shoulders, pretending not to get it, but I do. People connect over food. And pie is the perfect place to start.

They beam, deliver their homemade cards, and dash off to class parties of hot chocolate and gingerbread houses, wishing us a Merry Christmas and singing "Sleigh Ride" as they scurry out of sight. Mr. F watches me open the cards, and we read them together—simple notes of thanks and one hand-drawn picture of a flute with happy eighth notes surrounding it. I hang the art on the wall next to the poem I've already placed there. Then I open the bottom right-hand drawer of my desk and tuck their cards in the file folder buried there. Mr. F grins.

"I have one too," is all he says.

After winter recess, Rose brings Little Debbie Apple Pies for the entire jazz band, Mr. F, and me. I figure it's my turn, so I make a blueberry-peach pie and bring it to school. Mr. F and I share it, along with the unspoken acknowledgment that this is our new ritual, whether there is pie to be had or not. He knows I will not stop working unless he shows up to "talk shop," and from then on, he comes to my room every day.

One day, exasperated after continued frustrations with my seventh and eighth-grade band, I throw the score from the morning's rehearsal down on the table and launch into a detailed dramatization of the day's failures.

"My best eighth-grade clarinetist quit today. I can't get them to listen to me or the music. I can't explain the simplest rhythms, and we keep falling apart. I don't know what to do." I throw up my hands in defeat and sink into my chair.

Mr. F pulls the score across the table and scans it, peering into my problems.

"It's all right here," he says, pointing to the snare drum part.

He turns the score sideways so I can see. "Have your percussionist play this for everyone and it will work itself out."

I barely believe him, but now I am profoundly curious. It can't be that easy.

"Yes," he adds, as if hearing my thoughts. "It's that simple. Now go do it."

He hands back my score and I accept it, along with his challenge. Then I set to work on my salad, marking his advice in the margins between bites.

At the next morning's rehearsal, when we approach the measure in question, I stop.

"Folks, listen to this. Brendan, can you play your part for us?" And for the first time, they listen, because it's coming from one of them and not from me. They listen because they too are curious. He plays it perfectly. "Thank you. Now let's play it together, letting Brendan lead us."

We try it, and *Voila!* Mr. F was right. I see delighted surprise on the faces before me, and we play through the next section with the first bit of real feeling I've heard from them. I cannot wait until lunch to tell Mr. F, and I burst into his room just moments after the bell to recount our rehearsal. He leans back in his desk chair, arms crossed in front of him, and listens to my monologue. My voice—a little too loud, still projecting from class—is wild with the enthusiasm of my first small, but significant success.

Now every meal begins the same way: "It worked! Now what about this?"

I come to lunch hungry for my next lesson, and somehow every time, in one sentence, he gets to the heart of the matter, making what once seemed complicated easy. I have so many questions, but I limit myself to one a day, afraid to ask for more before I've successfully completed the assignment I've already been given. It becomes our great and ongoing game. I earn each piece of advice, and it always ends with his words, "It's simple. Now go do it."

The morning after our February jazz concert, I stop at a local coffee shop to buy some doughnut holes for the jazz band to enjoy while we review our performance. Buses arrive as I prepare the reflection form and a modest doughnut bar. I've just finished when the seventh and eighth-grade jazzers drag themselves, bleary eyed, to their seats. I pass out the papers and they accept them, thankful in their unusually low-energy state for the tradition of not playing the day after their concert.

That's when they see the doughnuts. Suddenly everyone seems happily caffeinated. It has the same effect as pie, and I silently thank Mr. F for the gambit as I pass around napkins. They each take two spheres of deep-fried, sugary perfection, and we listen to the recording, sharing successes, celebrating each other, and smiling with sweetness still on our lips.

As we wrap up, I encourage them to find someone to give a special shout out to.

"It can be anyone," I say. "Just take the time to tell them."

With the last few minutes of class, I clean up what remains of breakfast to a chorus of compliments.

"Your solo was so awesome!"

"Yours too!"

"Did you hear the high school band?"

"Yeah, their drummer is amazing!"

As I take the box to the trash, I see one leftover doughnut hole and decide to take my own advice.

Standing by the shelves at the front of the room near his own instrument is a shy saxophonist. He's been well trained by my predecessor and is well-mannered on his own accord. He lives and works on a local dairy farm, proudly wearing blue jeans, Timberland boots, and a green John Deere hoodie almost every day. His looks have been neither mean nor friendly. He's been one of the ones who simply didn't know what to think of me yet.

"Hey, Thomas," I say. "You want the last one?"

"Sure! Thanks!" he replies, taking it from the box.

"You know, I've been impressed by you all year. I'd love to hear you take a solo at the next concert," I say.

He seems surprised, but I can see by the smile at the corners of his eyes that he has accepted his assignment. The bell rings, and our time is up. I hear shouts of "thank you for the doughnuts!" over our banging door as they leave to take on the day. The last one to leave is the Farm Boy, Thomas. He waves his thanks and closes the door quietly behind him. In my empty room once more, I realize the strangers who entered it are now gone, and even though I haven't won them all over yet, I've won one more than before.

Despite the doughnuts, kids quit, rehearsals are rough, and we do not win gold at our festivals in my first year as middle school director. I don't know if Mr. F reached out because he saw my struggles or because he too was empty, missing Mr. Bishop like I missed all I'd left. Regardless, we find missing pieces of music, advice, and pie in the shakeup, and he helps me believe I will get better at this.

Eventually, some student artwork adorns my walls, but I don't try to fill them faster. I am no longer intimidated by their wide-open emptiness because I know it just takes time and a little something sweet to fill it up.

It's that simple. Now go do it.

YEAR NINE

"If you can meet with Triumph and Disaster
And treat those two imposters just the same;"

~Rudyard Kipling

Dat Dere

MIDDLE SCHOOL SHENANIGANS CONTINUE, and my mentored meals are interrupted by the regularly scheduled program of "Finch & Friends," otherwise known as sixth-grade jazz band. Every Thursday, they flatten music stands into tables, transforming the band room into their café. In the beginning, Mr. F exits as they enter with their Styrofoam trays of state-supplied sustenance. But before long he lingers, watching the way I work their feral, chocolate-milk-infused enthusiasm. Eventually, he stays the entire time, digesting the difficulty of what I'm attempting.

Slowly, his guidance seeps away from the table and into all my rehearsals. Now he never stops teaching me. We talk in the hall between lessons, on the way to meetings, and in the fragments of time we find before and after scheduled school. We stand, never intending to talk for long, right arm crossed over left, weight shifted in the same stance. His impact imbues my every move.

In one of these important standing sessions, he floats an idea.

"Ya know, students are having an exceptionally difficult

time scheduling Jazz II next year."

Jazz II, our second high school jazz band, is a training ensemble for our elite Jazz I, one of the best bands in the state.

"We've always had a hard time scheduling it," he continues. "There were years when half of Jazz II had lunch at the same time as our rehearsals. It was a mess, with them coming in late, playing over their plates. Jazz I never has this problem because it's scheduled every other day, opposite the concert band." He looks at me over his crossed arms. "If Jazz II could be scheduled at the same time as Jazz I, it would alleviate this issue."

I can tell that he wants me to teach it. This both frightens and flatters me. I am still unsteady in middle school, not ready for more. But I'm also curious.

The next day welcomes another sixth-grade jazz jam, complete with crinkle fries and peanut butter and jelly.

"Really swish those sandwiches out of your mouths before you play!" I say, and a line forms at the fountain.

The yearly cleaning of these instruments is going to be unbelievably gross, I think as I straighten the stands for rehearsal. We tackle one section at a time, and we're just finding our groove in "The Second Line" when the bell interrupts us again.

"See ya next week!" I concede over the clatter of cases and lunchboxes. Rose and Ashton are the last ones out the door. Having just taken up the trumpet and saxophone respectively for jazz band, they both give me a thumbs up to let me know it's going well before darting out the door.

Mr. F and I stand in the middle of the room, arms crossed, as we watch them go. Then he turns to me.

"Ya know, that Jazz II conflict for next year is turning out to be a big issue. But I checked, and every affected student can take the class if we run it at the same time as Jazz I."

I have been dreading this moment, certain of his inevitable ask but not my answer or ability. I draw a long breath, and on my unprepared exhalation a response that cannot be mine enters the world through my lips.

"Ya know," I say over my own crossed arms, "I have a problem too. There is no good place for the sixth-grade jazz band. Right now, it's scheduled during their lunch. We start late and barely have enough time to accomplish anything."

He stares into the mirror he has made of me, unable to answer, looking as surprised as I feel. Once again, we are interrupted by the bell and a stream of incoming students. Back to work we go, but this time it is I who have cast the line. I worry all night that I have angered him, let him down by not taking his lead, or presumed too much by telling him what to teach, but the next day he arrives in my room unexpectedly early.

"Deal," he says determinately, putting out his hand—which I take with an immense sense of relief.

I look at him over our handshake as he maps out our new plan: "I'll teach sixth-grade jazz band when you teach seventh and eighth grade, and you'll teach Jazz II while I teach Jazz I."

Although I am reluctant to relinquish anything with sixth grade, my current comfort zone, it is my fear of failing the high schoolers that makes me tighten my grip. His hand meets mine with a strength and assurance that says, *You can do this.*

"Deal," I reply, feeling his confidence flow through me. Then, with uncharacteristic conviction I add, "Now go do it."

He raises his eyebrows, and I see a surprised smile settle upon his features. We release our grasp, and he heads off to propose this plan to our principals. Within weeks we hear they have accepted our suggestion, and when the next school year begins, I see my name atop Jazz II's roster.

Underclassmen predominate in the class, training for their eventual acceptance into Jazz I, but I am surprised to see a smattering of juniors and seniors as well. They are just as surprised to see me, having taken the course because their favorite teacher, Mr. F, usually leads it. I see their disappointment and, based on my experiences last year, I fully expect them to quit before the add/drop period is over.

I pass out folders anyway, telling them about the pieces Mr. F helped me pick. It appeases them that I am a steward of his teachings. I hand them the jazz mouthpieces and reeds he has recommended as Duke Ellington grooves "The A Train" onward from the speakers at the front of the room. Their toes tap and their scrutiny softens as they look over their parts in our arrangement of the same tune.

At lunch I convey my misgivings about Jazz II's wimpy instrumentation, waffling confidence, and low morale.

"When those things happened to me," Mr. F answers, "I always told them they were the second-best jazz band around."

Wait, this happened to him too? This single sentence reveals that my mentor, pedestal and all, has dealt with this same struggle, even though he seems invincible now.

"In Jazz II's best years," he says, "every seat was filled, and they played just one level lower than Jazz I at our yearly state NYSSMA festivals. They were as good as any other school's Jazz I."

He must know the course he's charting, showing me what's possible if I work hard and use what I have wisely. Although teaching jazz is not the route I had sought for myself as a classical flutist, I can feel the opportunity he's giving me. Unknown as this path may be, I want to explore it all the more because of its divergence from the one I planned for myself.

"Don't be afraid to pull up some of your hot-shot middle

schoolers," he says, "or ask some woodwinds to learn trombone to fill the empty seats at the end of your sections. It's your job to balance your band. Now go do it."

So I do, and with one quick call to the Finch home I've got Lynn Finch learning trombone and Julian embracing the opportunity to hang with high schoolers. When they join us, Thomas and the other saxophones nod their approval at the power in the new low-brass line. The band feels less lame with every student who joins, so I continue making calls. Soon I'm teaching a talented clarinetist named Leah how to play trombone as well, and two more flute players pick up the saxophone.

After one Jazz II rehearsal, down the hall I hear my first fourth graders, now seniors, singing the lyrics of Mel Tormé's sizzling standard "Dat Dere" with the rhythm section.

> *Hey Daddy, what's Dat Dere?*
> *And what's dat under dere?*
> *Oh Daddy, oh hey Daddy,*
> *Hey look at over dere!*
> *And what dey doing dere?*
> *And where dey go in dere?*

Not every band sings, but Mr. F's do. Curious, I head down the hall to see if I can collect another idea from him. He is coaching them through the lyrics to improve their interpretation of the phrases.

"This is intense music that needs your maturity. You've got to land on the words 'what' and 'where' because those are the words that change. Play the change," he says, and they do.

The night of our spring concert, these lyrics loiter in my

mind, and although I am excited to share our work with the audience, I am mostly concerned with what Mr. F will think. Jazz II begins, and the first piece sends a snapshot of our weekly work into the audience. Rhyse, Saoirse, and AJ sit right up front with Dan, as he encourages this trio of toddlers to clap at the right time. My band members smile at their enthusiasm as they pull forward the sheet music for their ballad. They play with a sensitivity their parents have not yet heard from them, and Thomas solos over the Finches' low harmonies. We end with a barn-burning swing chart. The saxes shred the soli they've been practicing for weeks, and six little feet swing along with them from the front seats of our theater.

Then Jazz I takes the stage, and the Jazz II underclassmen watch in awe, inspired by what awaits them. They are playing "Dat Dere" again, and the sneaky words worm their way into my mind.

> *My quizzical kid!*
> *Man, she doesn't want anything hid!*

Even after they are done, the insistent tune repeats in my mind. When the jazz students join forces with other band members for the concert band portion of the program, they groove just as hard as they did with the jazz charts. At the concert's conclusion, Mr. F and I take hands and bow with them.

> *She's forever demanding to know*
> *Who, what and why and where!*

Parents snap after-concert photos in front of the stage and congratulate their kids and us on another excellent concert. After everyone, even the lingerers have left, Mr. F turns to me.

"Listen, I have to talk to you," he says.

My heart beats faster, sensing the seriousness in his voice. Still euphoric from the success on stage, I prepare for some final praise, which is not something he has wasted much of on me.

Inquisitive child!
And sometimes her questions get wild!

"You can't let your rhythm section do that."
Do what? My mind is racing now.
"Your drummer is clearly not listening to your bassist."
This is not the nod I had hoped for.
"I could not even hear your guitarist."
This is what I was afraid of.
"And your piano player is way too loud."
Defeat.
"Actually, every one of them, except your inaudible guitarist, is too loud."

I feel like crying, but I don't. My ears burn from holding back my emotion.

"You can't let them do that."

Gotta tell her what she needs to know.

He goes on.

"Your rhythm section sounds like they have gone months without instruction from you. You need to tell them something in every rehearsal. Do not simply stick to your horn section because that is where you feel comfortable. The rhythm section is half your band. Pay attention to them. Tell them how they can be better; otherwise, they learn that you don't care, or worse—that they are perfect."

He must see me shrinking inside myself.

The time will march, the years will go.

"You want gold at festival, don't you?" His words bite.
The little lass is gonna grow.

He knows I want that success, and I feel like a fool for believing I might be good at this. I can't stand to think of myself going into all those rehearsals, missing all these things. What is my conservatory training worth if my basic musicianship has missed these obvious problems?

Help her along...

"Yes," I say, dealing with this information and trying not to show my shame in letting him down.

So she'll know right from wrong.

"Well, go do it," he barks.

Gotta make her strong.

I am dumbstruck. I want to hide. I want to quit. But the festival is in fourteen days, and he clearly thinks that's enough time to correct our course.

I swallow my pride and decide to buckle down. Over the next two weeks, we work harder than ever. I stop the band at every breath, pulling the rhythm section into everything we've honed with the horns. He was right. They soak in my every suggestion. They are hungry to be seen.

I've been such a fool, but nothing would be more foolish than remaining so.

We are all struck by how much can be accomplished after a concert. I only wish I did it all sooner. When the festival finally comes, I cannot sleep the night before. My mind races with music and mishaps.

The time will march, the years will go.

I am sure my band members can see my nerves as we take the stage, which I know is no good, but they play their parts with a new maturity.

"I don't know, but I think our piano dynamics were the quietest I have ever heard them," Thomas says when we leave the adjudication room.

"We didn't lose time either, like we usually do," adds Lynn.

"Yeah, I think we could have stayed on the backside of the beat more in the last tune, but that's about it," Julian adds.

These three sound like music teachers, talking shop just like Mr. F and me.

We wait for our scores for what seems like hours, even though the clock says only twenty minutes have passed. Julian, Thomas, and Lynn are there when I turn the plaque over in my hand. They jump up when they see it and run off to tell everyone else that Jazz II got gold.

The little lass is gonna grow.

It's not just Jazz II. This year our school has sent eleven groups to compete, and every one of us gets gold.

The plaque goes on the wall outside the band room, but I tuck a copy of "Dat Dere" into the manila student file in my drawer. From the outside we look so strong, but somehow I still feel sheepish. I fear I cannot do this without Mr. F, and I am even more afraid that he thinks so too. So instead of sinking into satisfaction, Mr. F and I dive into the fathoms, to deal with all the things I do not know.

YEAR TEN

*"If you can bear to hear the truth you've spoken
Twisted by knaves to make a trap for fools,"*

~Rudyard Kipling

Passing the Baton

THE NEXT SUMMER IS SEAMLESS. We never stop, as we dive headfirst into the sea of my shortcomings—which is predominantly percussion. Mr. F introduces me to these varied creatures in the back of my band room through his sets of compulsory summer chores.

"Vibrations from a year of playing loosen the tension rods and knots," he says. "Every summer you should tighten them."

Another assignment. I adopt it dutifully.

My room is a smaller, hand-me-down copy of the high school room. So each chore he models in his, I mimic in mine. We re-head every worn drum. I shadow the star pattern he shows me to evenly tune them, carefully matching the pitch of each node with the drum key he gives me.

"Add that to your key ring," he instructs. "A good director is never without one."

It feels more like a gift than an assignment as I affix it to the lanyard around my neck. It's as though I've been knighted, and with this addition the sounds of my steps jangle differently down the hall. They sound more like his.

Along our way, he tells me each instrument's story, the

circumstances in which he found or purchased them: the special-order snares, the custom-made frame for his rescued rosewood bars, the beautiful resonator box the bells sit in. Nothing here is an accident, and it's all by his doing. His hands sail easily through familiar motions as he speaks, while mine fumble for their first time. His movements are assured, while my touch is tentative, wary of making any issue worse.

"It is not broken beyond your means," he says with a lighthearted shrug. "Go on. Do it."

He shows me knots that will not slip, and with them we re-string wind chimes, tubular bells, gongs, and xylophone bars. After several sets of cymbal knots, my fingers begin to trace the patterns with an echo of his ease. We level pedals and tighten every joint of our stands and drum sets, so our students will see them as new.

We inventory every instrument. He determines replacement plans, I log details, and we repair every crooked key along the way. We examine each piece in our jazz library, and he discards outdated charts while I update our spreadsheet with his notes. He points out every piece that is a "winner," and I mark them with asterisks, illuminating our inventory with little stars.

"Mr. Bishop and I combined our jazz libraries a few years ago," he tells me. "We intended to do the same for our concert band libraries, but you'll need to do that, just like we are doing today."

He looks at me and I know I have received an assignment for some time far in the future. I feel in the way he holds himself that we will not do this one together.

"Don't worry," I say. "I'll do it."

It is a promise, and we both feel it.

"I know you will," he says, putting "Quiet Night of Quiet Stars" back in its box while I add another asterisk.

After our last summer lesson, he turns to me. "Arthur and Anne have been accepted to All-State this year."

"Oh, that's wonderful!" I reply.

"Yes, it is, but I'll be chairing the Conference's All-State Jazz Ensemble. So I thought you might like to be their official chaperone because you started them."

"Yes," I say. "I would love that."

Fall is fantastic. The middle school bands are now full of students I know from my time at the elementary school, and I enjoy the extra time I get with all these groups. Eighth grade suits my pre-K clan. They are finally middle school's big fish. I can't believe how far they've come from "Hot Cross Buns." I practice every night to stay ahead of them.

My kids get a kick out of my at-home practice sessions. So when they inevitably interrupt me, I teach them a little of each instrument. They are still too small to hold them properly, but I help them make their first sounds on each one. Their attempts are silly and short-lived. Soon they are back to playing with their toys by my feet while I practice eighth-grade band music and level-five festival solos. Over dinner, the kids hum the band music from their booster seats, which my husband finds hysterical. I love every lesson and only wish I could hang on to these moments longer.

In December, Arthur, Anne, and I head up to All-State, passing the forgotten fireman statue on our way out of town. He holds his lantern and the child tight, though still no one seems to care that his fountain is dry and his paint is peeling away.

Between professional development sessions, I sit in the back of the All-State rehearsals and watch the conductors, Arthur, Anne, and Mr. F at work. They are elated in this world of exceptional music-making, and I am reminded of how life-altering these events were for me too. As a high school flutist at this same convention center, I discovered a level of music-making more passionate and perfect than I had yet known. I feel that way again.

After dinner, I wander the exhibit hall and find myself at a booth filled with Frank Battisti books. There is a new one I haven't read yet, so I buy it and head back to my hotel room. There I write notes of congratulations to Arthur and Anne, and while my pen glides over my paper, I feel how much I have missed not being their teacher every day. It is so sweet to have started them, and so poignant to be here at their end. But there is a pang of missing the middle that fills me more than ever before.

I seal their letters and climb into bed. Snuggled among an obscene amount of hotel pillows, I pull out Mr. Battisti's new book and read myself to sleep.

I meet Mr. F in the mezzanine for the final marathon of All-State performances, and we clap for the choir, for Anne in the band, and finally for Arthur with the symphony orchestra. The strings and the brass open their portion of the program with the fanfare of Berlioz's "Roman Carnival," but it is Liszt's "Les Préludes" that moves me. I look down and see Julian enraptured by the music, like he was at that first concert with Mrs. Darling, and I know I don't want to miss a single step with my Three Musketeers.

Keeping up with Mr. F is hard, but I love being his sidekick, and our students excel more than ever under our shared direction. After our own February jazz concert is over, and the waves of audience recede, we cross our arms in conversation by the middle school band room doors. I know now to be prepared for the unfiltered feedback he gives me after each performance. I am accustomed to the way it bites through the soft spots of my thickening shell.

"You know..." he starts, and I brace myself... "Our jazz deal was the best thing we ever did for this program."

Is this praise? I want to say something meaningful, but all I can muster is a lame, "Yeah...."

"I have to tell you something," he continues.

Ah, here it comes: all the things I've missed and my next assignment.

"I'm retiring at the end of this year."

The wheels of my mind grind to a halt.

He can't leave. If the last year has proved anything, it's that I need his guidance. He tells me what to do and I do it. *That's* our deal.

"But you can't leave now. We've just started," I say, feeling like my life's been interrupted by school's tolling bell.

"I am. The time is right. I'll still be working at the University. I'm not done making music."

I can't deal with this. I am surprised by the strength of my sadness. This bell rings for him, not me. I have been training to take on his position, and he and I both know it. I just hoped we would have just a little more time. I want him to tell me I am ready to take the job, but he doesn't. This moment is about his retirement, and he's leaving that decision up to me.

On the drive home, I encourage myself to be happy for him and I focus on the opportunity I now have to move up with my pre-K clan again. I've always wanted to stay with them, and right before me is the opportunity. It would mean many more concerts, with much harder music to prepare. I'd also have the added time commitment of directing the musical and the marching band. Not to mention, I'd be signing myself up for another year of feeling like a first-year teacher, with new lesson plans to write and new pedagogies to master.

It would certainly be a lot for me to take on with young kids, but by the time I walk in my front door I'm feeling energized by the idea. I'm ready to talk to Dan about the added responsibility and time commitments, and what it would mean for our family.

But when I find Dan, he's sitting at the dining room table, head in his hands. Something is wrong.

"Is everything okay?" I ask.

He lifts his head. "I'm not sure. Today when I dropped Saoirse off at preschool, AJ kept saying his stomach hurt. They couldn't get him calmed down, so they took him to the pediatrician. But the pediatrician sent them to the emergency room, and the emergency room sent them to Upstate Children's Hospital. They are there now, going through all kinds of testing. They don't know what's wrong...but I'm just so worried. Something doesn't feel right."

I don't mention Mr. F's retirement or the job.

I can think of nothing besides AJ and our family, but there is no waiting at school. Mr. F makes his big announcement, and everyone's reaction is the same: "No one could ever fill those shoes." I am embarrassed by the way those words hurt me and by how unhappy I am in his hour of celebration. I'm still reeling when Arthur, Jeremiah, Leah, and Thomas enter my room on a mission.

"We have to do something special for Mr. F at his last concert," Thomas explains.

"What do you have in mind?" I say, trying to mask the worry in my own.

"We're getting him gifts, but can you invite alumni to come play with us?" asks Leah.

"Well, I don't know them all, but I can write an email. We'll share it and see who comes."

"Great! We'll forward it to the alumni we know too," Jeremiah says.

"We have to pick a song everyone knows, since we won't be able to rehearse without him finding out."

"Sleigh Ride," Arthur says without a doubt. "We play it every year. Everyone knows it, and he loves it."

They all agree. It's the perfect choice.

Over the next few weeks, countless alumni respond to our call. Mr. F asks Julian to join the high school band for the spring concert, and he stays after school with me to learn the third trombone part to "Fiesta!," Mr. F's favorite piece besides "Sleigh Ride." All the bands practice harder than ever, knowing this is Mr. F's last concert. It feels the same with my pre-K class. It's our last performance together before they move to the high school, and my heart is aching even more with the thought of passing them on to someone besides my mentor.

At the spring concert, during Mr. F's traditional senior recognition speech, we sneak the alumni on stage behind the curtain. The seniors present Mr. F with their gifts, and then I hear them say, "But wait, we have one more."

That's our cue. I point to the student standing ready at the ropes and our big blue curtain swings open as we start "Sleigh Ride."

Emotion fills Mr. F's face as he takes it in—a band of the students that mattered most to him sitting on the stage, waiting for him to lead them one last time. I gesture for him to take his place on the podium in front of them. He silently mouths, "Thank you," as the baton passes from my hand to his.

No one misses a beat at the transition. Seamless. The way it should be.

After the music ends, alumni relate how Mr. F's impact far

outlasted their time in his classroom. He accepts each anecdote, and knowing there are countless more, we encourage everyone to join us in the cafeteria to share stories, and of course—pie! We loiter for a long time, taking it all in, and before I leave for the night, I place the concert program in my right-side file.

With his successful send-off completed, my mind returns to my family and the decision I have to make. AJ's dad had called the night after he left school to say that the test results had come back. Dan was quiet on the phone, and when he got off he took my hand and said, "AJ has been diagnosed with cancer."

We still have no idea what the future holds for him. He is three. He doesn't even know what the word cancer means. My kids don't know either, when my husband and I try to explain it to them.

There is no other priority. I must be there for my family.

All I want is to protect the people I love from the scary future I see. So I choose a course I believe is best, even though it's not what I want. I choose not to follow my pre-K clan. *They should have a new teacher anyway,* I tell myself. *It's best for everyone.*

Back at school, I tell Mr. F and my colleagues why I can't take the job. They are stunned when I tell them about AJ, and they say they understand. I want Mr. F to tell me it will be okay, that AJ will be okay, and I should just take the job. But he doesn't. He respects my decision.

When they post the high school position, applications don't pour in. No one wants to fill Mr. F's enormous shoes. Thankfully, one promising candidate submits an impressive résumé and wins the job, but as I walk away from the interview, I have a sinking feeling.

The new teacher, Ms. Ismay, comes to watch our last concert of the year. She meets the students and congratulates Mr. F. She does all the right things, and so do I. But not even the most skilled sailor can stop a storm.

After graduation's fanfare of "Pomp and Circumstance," Mr. F and I stand, arms crossed, in the band room. I am both stunned that it is time to watch him go and torn over the opportunity that is passing me by. I have wondered constantly if I am disappointing him.

"Here," he says, extending his hand. He places his keys in my open palm, and I feel how hard this is for him.

"Write it down," he says as he looks to where his band should be. "Write down their names, and where you took them, and the pieces you played. Write it all down so you remember."

"I will," I promise.

"I know," he says. Then I watch him walk away while a distant train rumbles once more across its trodden tracks.

YEAR ELEVEN

"Or watch the things you gave your life to, broken,
And stoop and build 'em up with worn-out tools;"

~Rudyard Kipling

The Only Way Out Is Through

THE NEXT YEAR IS STORMY right from the start. The school's addition of new electives forces major changes in how we group our bands. Despite my warnings, the changes happen anyway, hastily redirecting our carefully charted courses. So quickly we are lost without our Captain. Additionally, Ms. Ismay—now at the helm—does little to avoid turbulent waters. She doesn't play to our strengths; she sees our inadequacies and steers straight for them.

"These students cannot sight read well," she tells me. "They need to focus on fundamentals. There is so much remedial work we need to do."

Her list of grievances goes on. Our students are excellent listeners and players of elements that are off the page, but it's true: Many of our younger players still need work on reading. I can't help but feel like this is my fault.

I know she's right about the work we need to do, but with all the recent changes, now is the wrong time to home in on their faults. I take every action I can to protect the bands, but over the fall, students quit in droves. They leave, clinging to their devotion to Mr. F and the memory of something they no longer perceive as possible. I beg parents, but it's no use. Our program is falling apart before my eyes. And I can't help but feel like this is my fault too.

At home, we miss seeing AJ, since he is at the children's hospital so often receiving treatment. My children send him cards, and we mask up to see him when we can. By the holidays, he has completed chemo, radiation, and surgery. The doctors say it is time to let him rest, before his next round of treatments, and that if there is anything we would like to do with him, we should do it now.

We should have known what that meant.

At Christmas, my family gathers together, singing songs and sharing gifts, but we feel cancer's presence at our table— a shadow over all of us. As we snuggle up for stories by the tree, Rhyse and Saoirse are careful of AJ's port. His gifts are games he can play while getting his treatments. With everything the doctors have done, we truly believe he'll make it, but in January the doctors cancel his treatment and move him to hospice.

Less than two weeks later—as I am working in my band room to the sounds of Saturday set build, with my children at my feet—comes the call. "AJ is gone," Dan tells me. Everyone will be at our house when we get home. My children look at me as I hang up, and I know they already know. So I tell them by the whiteboard they once drew their dreams upon that their best friend is gone. I hold their little bodies, limp and soaked in anguish.

I can hardly hold myself together as we drive home, past the statue—now rusted and decrepit. His base is held together with flimsy zip ties, but he's still holding the child despite the difficulties they both endure.

The wailing I expected is silence instead. The house holds

people, but no one says a word. For the first time in my life, I feel grown, holding up my whole house, cradling the unimaginable grief of our children and our parents at the same time. Everyone on all sides of me is suffering. No one moves to turn on the lights as evening comes.

I try not to speak of it at school, but when a child dies everyone knows. It lives like a mark burned across bloodshot eyes that everyone sees but cannot acknowledge. Unutterable agony. Miss Garnet hugs me in the hall, and I can't help but cry, releasing the pain of the people he left and the injustice of cancer's torment of a toddler. I told my students he was sick, but I can't bring myself to tell them what has happened now— and none of them ask.

Mr. F stops by after his University rehearsal, and I tell him I must play at the funeral.

"How am I supposed to do this?" I ask.

"You can. Musicians do it all the time. You know how. Put your grief in a box and get the job done. You can open the box later, anytime you need to."

So simple. He calms me, and I do it. Just like he said. Dan and I play "Blackbird" and "I Am Weary" for AJ and our family at his funeral, and at night I hear Saoirse singing herself to sleep with these songs.

A month later, Mr. F comes back to play in the musical, and sees, to my embarrassment, what we have become without him. Standing at the edge of the dropped pit in front of our stage, I look down at his drum set, a view I nearly never have. I see his red disappointment creep up the sides of his neck.

Everything I've tried to avoid has happened this year. I feel like I should have taken the job and stayed with the class I started with. Maybe at least now I would be where I was supposed to be. None of my choices feel like the right ones. None of them changed the outcome. AJ didn't make it, and the program is in shambles. Everything is ruined, and I didn't protect anyone. Regret surges through me.

"I made a mistake," I tell him.

He looks up at me from the pit.

"I know," he says. I feel the lash of letting him down once again, until I see the searing pain I've recently come to know in his eyes as well. Then he adds so softly only I can hear, "I know how it feels."

Flash Floods & Forests

FROM JANUARY THROUGH APRIL, I feel hopeless. My family mourns, and things continue to worsen at school. We miss AJ. Everything reminds us of him. I've missed my chance. And now I'm missing the ninth grade with my pre-K class. Time moves slowly, and I feel lost, with no relief in sight. Everything feels wrong.

My own rehearsals feel arid and lifeless, and the students dislike the new schedule. They come to rehearsal with morale even lower than mine. I fear we are one step away from mutiny. After one dismal spring rehearsal, I am standing at the door—reciting "Have a good day" like an aspirational prayer as they leave—when I look down the hall to see Thomas walking toward me.

"How's it going?" I ask. He is the perennial spokesperson for positivity, so when his answer is "Ehh," I know the well of his own enthusiasm is also low.

"Would you maybe be able to coach me on a jazz solo for the NYSSMA festival this year?" he asks.

I don't hesitate. "Yes, of course," I say, and his demeanor lifts a little. "When's a good time for you?"

"Maybe before school, if that works for you. I have practice after."

We set up a time, and he comes in for lessons on Friday mornings while it is still dark. We choose a solo based on the rhythm changes—a rite of passage for any advancing jazzer. Despite our program's struggles, he has made good progress. Having missed the fall with him, I can hear his improvement more acutely.

For weeks we work on the solo together, inching up the speed click by click on the metronome until we approach performance tempo. We treat it like a video game, and every time I advance the tempo I announce, *"Level up!"* He laughs even though I am pushing him out of his comfort zone. As his skills start to surpass mine, I play less and less. I might feel inadequate at this, but I am so happy to share the lesson that I no longer care.

A few weeks before the festival, he comes in as scheduled for his morning lesson.

"Today I think you should play the whole thing for me," I say. He rolls his head back, ready to resist so I shout, *"LEVEL UP!"* with a laugh. He smiles, picks up his saxophone, and does as I ask. I just listen, and when he's done, I ask, "So what do you think?"

That's all it takes for it all to come spilling out: his opinions, ideas, frustrations. He critiques each measure, sharing his own inadequacies and making me feel more at home with my own.

"And wow," he finishes, "the lick at the turnaround gets me every time." He runs his hand through his blond hair in exasperation.

There is no need for me to share my assessment. He has said all I would have and more. I suppose I could contrive some final exercises, but instead I choose to offer him an opportunity: "Would you like to try it again?" I ask.

He looks at the music and then at me before shouting, *"LEVEL UP!"* Then he takes up his saxophone again and answers with a version of his solo that is all his. Freed from pleasing others—even me—he makes his own choices about the music, and he makes them happen. I have done almost nothing, but we both leave the lesson appreciating each other more than ever.

In April, Ms. Ismay and I realize that enrollment for the next year is down considerably. Not long after, she announces she's accepted another job closer to home. She will be leaving at the end of the year. I still wish I could have helped her more. We were all doing our best. Students would have quit this year, and cancer would have come no matter what we did. Some years are like that.

So we pass the baton again. And this time, I take it up at first offer, thankful and unafraid. Living through everything you thought you couldn't does that. Marooned at sea, without fresh water, somehow you survive. And when life offers you a glass, you take it, and drink, and water becomes something sweet and sacred upon your lips because of what you were without it. When you've known this thirst, the first glass is rapture. No one could have told me or my students to be thankful for this. We had to be thirsty first.

Taking the baton this time is like that—a glass of hope in my hand, an apology for the choice I couldn't make before. The students accept it, and I hear nothing more about shoes I cannot fill. For May and June, even though Ms. Ismay is still there, I take on the extra duties of the high school position, thankful for the distraction they provide from the pain I'm still feeling. I teach marching basics to the parade band and students start re-enrolling for next year.

We take our rehearsals outside, and one day we march past

the beautiful new elementary school, now full of children. Kindergarteners run to the windows to see us march on by, and they wave in excitement at our impromptu parade.

On Memorial Day, we march past the fireman's fountain, but there's something new...a big purple sign nearby. When the remembrance ceremony at the courthouse has concluded and the band is loading the buses, I walk back over to him. His paint has flaked away, and no water runs from his rust-filled fountain. He is broken but still here.

And on his purple sign, I read that our Fire Department has taken on his restoration. I read further:

The fountain was given to the Village and its firefighters in 1914 by Frank M. Baker as a memorial to his son, George Hobart Baker, who was killed in an automobile accident in 1913. Both men had been members and chief engineers of the Fire Department. The fountain, depicting a fireman holding a baby, is a symbol of the Valley and its community-minded residents.

I walk slowly back to the buses with a feeling I haven't felt all year creeping back to me. Each step, a sip.

"You try spitting out all these words at that tempo and see how you like it!" Ashton spits into her microphone.

It is August and the high school rock band is working, somewhat unsuccessfully, through their first evening rehearsal. The new middle school director and I have spent all summer taking the students' requests and writing arrangements. But we're stumbling into every pitfall because I do not know how to avoid them—or even that they exist. Just setting up the sound system presented major obstacles for me. In this tech-heavy world, I don't know what I don't know— like the difference between a monitor and a speaker, and who knows what else. Fortunately, I've found some answers on the internet (what a wonderful wellspring) and texted Mr. F my remaining questions. I trust him more than a search engine, and he always writes back.

Our attempt at Stevie Wonder's iconic "Signed, Sealed, Delivered (I'm Yours)" has come apart at the seams—again. The horns howled past any semblance of balance reaching for the rangy notes of the intro, while the rest of the rhythm section stumbled through a minefield of flats. James is on the drum set next to Leah, who has learned bass. And together in their unregulated enthusiasm, they took a tempo beyond all possible diction. But Ashton—now the band's most impressive lead singer—is not taking any tempos that aren't hers. We weren't more than eight bars in when the singers called these renegades back to reality with a screeching halt.

"That was way too fast!" Ashton goes on.

"I can't even hear my backup vocals," Lynn adds, glaring at Ben the guitarist and Matthew on keys, who are both frantically noodling, still trying to find their flats. These musicians have been around enough rehearsals to have opinions on how they should go.

"Maybe if you actually memorized your words, you could keep up with us," Rose counters, trumpet in hand, muscles taught under the sleeves of her graphic tee. The room is tense.

"Okay," I step in. "Where should we pick up?"

"The first verse," the vocalists immediately agree.

"Oh? And what bar is that?" the horns prod back, still activated and edgy.

Lining up the form between the lead sheet and sheet music has already been a hurdle for us. Luckily, Leah is positioned to defuse the standoff.

"It's bar five, guys," she says matter-of-factly, saving the entire band from implosion.

"She's amazing," says Julian, helping to further ease the

tension. "She always knows where we are, even when we don't." James and Matthew nod with respect in Leah's direction.

I laugh. Then they all do too, finally letting go of the strain we felt building over all of last year. I don't even care that I've never worked with this kind of ensemble before, and honestly know nothing. I'm happy to serve and to add a few arrangements to Mr. F's prolific library of pop tunes.

"Why don't you all take a few minutes, practice your parts on your own, get a drink if you need it," I suggest. "We'll start up again in five."

They do and we try it again, coming to a compromise that offers each section what they need to make it work. We don't let inexperience stop us, and we don't hang on to what isn't working. We are finally doing it, owning our messy, wind-rough hair because it's ours. Rehearsals might not be efficient, but finally they're fun and they're free and they're just what we need.

As these summer evenings break, the rains come unexpectedly, in sideways sheets. It is during one of these storms, with no one else in the building, that I release the reins of the rock band. My Three Musketeers jam alongside Thomas, Rose, and Leah, taking each other's lead with little looks as the rain pounds at our windows. As Ashton and Lynn sing, I am outside myself—remembering what they once were, while I witness their discovery of who they are and what they might become. Finally, I am not so afraid that all my first failures will inevitably ruin them.

Suddenly, our phones pinged with flash flood warnings and parents call their children in concern. We all have a little PTSD about raging rainstorms and rising waters. I dismiss them early and stay at the school in case they can't get home. The Finch parents arrive to pick up their children and (of course) insist on staying with me to make sure my little car can make it through the waters roaring off the hill. And it's a good thing they do. When we hear the rest have made it and head for the main road, my way home is temporarily unpassable.

"We planned for James to spend the night," the Finches tell me. "We already have an air mattress on the floor." Mr. Finch says, "Why don't you stay?" I feel that I'm making an awkward imposition, but it feels even stranger to sleep at school, so I accept their offer.

The path to their house is drenched but navigable. Once we make it there, I call my husband to tell him I'm okay, then fall asleep on their first floor to the sounds of video game glory above me. In the morning, I wake before everyone, as I always do. Quietly, I leave with a note of thanks on their round kitchen table. Then I text my husband and head back to school to tidy up a few things left out from last night.

Remnants of the woods' uprooted soil are washed up on the road with scattered sticks and acorns, but other than that we have escaped unscathed. The storm was strong and short and over. I arrive to find the band room still smelling like last night's rehearsal—sweaty and sweet, growing with good things that are not yet ready for the rest of the world. I tidy scattered sheets of music in the warm morning light and feel it feeding the grass in the field outside my window. Green and gushing from last night's storm, the earth accepts the sun, ready with water in reserve.

"Wait, who has the ball now?" I ask James as our first home game begins under the lights. I am stumbling through football season and pep band just like I did with the rock band.

"We do!" He laughs, along with the other sophomore

members of the drumline. "We won the coin toss." The sun is setting over a few scattered oak trees at the far edge of the field, tinting the clouds a spectacular pink.

"See that little football on the scoreboard?" Dan chimes in, and I nod. "When it's next to the word 'home,' we have the ball." He is playing trumpet and serving as our unofficial brass coach and football consultant. Rhyse wears the smallest bass drum, and Saoirse wields a light-up tambourine. Together we give a new meaning to the phrase "family band."

"Oh, excellent. That is very helpful!" I say in all sincerity, and the entire band laughs.

The announcer's voice booms over the speaker.

"And that's another ten yards for the Valley!" says Mr. Devens. He's the high school public speaking teacher and basketball coach, and he's been the voice of our football games for as long as anyone can remember.

"We're within scoring distance now," James explains. "We should get ready with the 'Fight Song.'"

"Number One next," I call out and the entire pep band quickly flips to the front of their binders. I write a big numeral one on the whiteboard by my side and hold it up for the students in the back to see in case they didn't hear me. Play progresses and I can barely see what is happening over the heads of the players on the sidelines.

"Let's go, Thomas!" Julian and Lynn call from the trombone section. Thomas isn't playing sax with us because he's playing left tackle for the varsity team.

"Touchdown!" Leah exclaims from the clarinet section.

"Play it!" Dan confirms with a wave of his hand. Rose and Ashton are right beside him, ready and exuberant with their instruments in playing position.

"One, two, three, four!" I shout, and the band is racing through the fight song as the players line up to kick their extra point.

The game goes on and the wind whips colder across our shoulders, but we are warm from cheering for our winning team. When the game is over, the band members, our families, and I haul our gear back to the room. There, on the other side of the school, we sip hot chocolate and wait for everyone to get picked up. After the last students have left, my family and I walk to our cars, arms full of extra coats and blankets.

"Hey look," Saoirse says right outside the band room door, "an acorn!"

She picks it up like it's a present.

"Yeah, but where did it come from?" I ask, looking over at Dan.

"There are no oak trees here," he adds.

"Maybe an absent-minded squirrel dropped it," Rhyse says, and we laugh.

"Probably," we agree.

"Well, I think it's the perfect place for a tree," says Saoirse and she bends down and presses it into the soft earth outside the band room door where it landed.

The whole year is like that. So bright it blinds my memories. I lead the music, and my students lead me. They make sure the best parts of what Mr. F started don't get lost in the fumble between teachers, and we rescue each other over and over. I drop the ball far too many times, but I am happy, in a way I never thought I could be after all that has happened. I learn things, not so methodically as Mr. F would have taught me, but in the wild way the world rushes at the wind. I am blown back and forth, finally settling where I should have been—a thirsty acorn in a field that might one day be forest.

YEAR TWELVE

"If you can make one heap of all your winnings
And risk it on one turn of pitch-and-toss,"

~Rudyard Kipling

Becoming A Conductor

ALL YEAR, I CONTINUE to let myself live in that wild way, with happiness unchecked. There is so much I am thankful for, so much to learn every day. Our clarinetist Leah is accepted to All-State, and I watch her rehearsals there while taking notes to improve my own. Her concert is just as moving as Arthur's and Anne's. I sit by Mr. F to share her success, just as we did when we worked together. At the conference, it's easy to forget that we no longer do.

"I know you've got the spring all planned out," he says as we walk to our cars after the concert, "but what are your plans for the summer?"

"Well, I've been thinking about applying to a summer conducting clinic with Frank Battisti," I admit. "I probably won't get in. It's geared toward doctoral students and professional conductors, but I want to try. I'd love to see him work with a group now that I've read everything he's written."

"You should," Mr. F replies.

So I risk an application, and to my delighted surprise, I'm accepted. I tell my family by asking my mother how this workshop might fit in with our summer vacation plans.

"Boston in August is perfect," she says. "We can drive right up after your father's heart checkup at Mount Sinai."

I tell Mr. F by asking him for help preparing. He works with graduate conducting students at the University, so this should be right up his alley. He accepts, of course, and we meet in the rare suspension of time known as Sundays in summer.

Back in our old room, he sits before me—posing as my band—and I sing out the melody, accenting the entrances I'm looking for.

"Okay." He waves his hand, stopping me. "We have a lot of work to do." He massages his brain through his brow as he ponders where to possibly begin.

"Here," he says. "Just show me how you hold it."

I do.

"It's all wrong."

Of course it is.

"There is no future in it, because you are too tight," he continues. "You're going to get too good at doing it poorly. You'll be able to conduct plenty of music like that, until one day you find yourself unable to proceed—either injured from bad mechanics or too rigid to navigate demanding passages."

"Here, like this." His voice softens as he takes his own baton. "Relax your grip." As he shows me, I see the countless times he's done this, how naturally the stick sits in his hands, like it loves to be there, an extension of him.

Once we get my setup squared away, we actually talk about music.

"They don't need you to conduct the melody. Everyone knows it."

"What should I conduct then?"

I get the look.

"Whatever they need."

He waits around his words. Musicians call this articulatory

silence: a deliberate space left around notes needing extra emphasis, which volume and attack alone could never provide.

Then he adds, "Honestly, choose anything else."

I try again and again, putting my untested ideas out there, and after every phrase he hones my setup, centering my stance and slicing away at every stray movement.

"Any motion you do not intend detracts from the one you do. These distractions teach your players that your movements mean nothing. Activate only your wrist. Do not give away your power. It's leaking out your elbow."

I center myself again, singing anything but the melody and cuing the invisible band before me with calculated wrist flicks any fencer would envy.

He sighs, stands, and walks toward me. "Remember to level your ictus like we talked about. Now, how many bars is that last phrase?"

"Twelve?" I say, fearing this is a trick question.

"Good. And the next?"

"Another twelve?" I reply with increasing conviction.

"Yes, and after that?"

"Eleven?" Each incarcerated syllable squeezes through the bars of my teeth.

"Precisely. And you are afraid of it."

How does he always know?

"You are looking down. The page will not protect you, and the music can't stay there. You must pull it from your players."

He looks at me, exemplifying the very technique he is training me in.

"Okay," I say with the determined voice of a toddler untethering her training wheels.

I level my stance and shoulders again.

"Just memorize those phrase lengths and look up," he

encourages. "It's easy and important. Conduct the page to your people."

Then he swipes the stand from me. Nothing but air is between us now and I feel the enormity of it, my safety net gone. I close my eyes for a moment, breathe, and raise my wand in the ritual he has rooted in me. I imagine the faces of my band members, and I sing a countermelody from the horn part, then a driving backbeat from the trombones and snare. I move with those meanings instead.

"Better," he breathes. "Now you know how much memorizing you have to do and why you must do it."

"Yes," I answer. "You can't conduct with only one connection."

Studying scores consumes my summer, and I leave for Boston's cityscape with my family, Mr. F's markings on my music and his motions in my mind. He has freed me from my unintended habits, along with the beliefs they grew from—limits I no longer need. I am propelled forward by the prospect of meeting the man behind the books that have encouraged my interest in improving for so many years.

My father's heart valve checkup in New York City goes well, and my parents meet us in Boston for vacation the week before the clinic. Much of the city has changed since my time there in college, but the brass ducklings in the Public Gardens have not. Saoirse and Rhyse are delighted to see ducks—real and brass—as well as the Swan Boats from their picture books, in real life. I feel the same way a week later as I walk into the conservatory's performance hall and see Mr. Battisti, the author of my favorite books, waiting for the symposium to begin.

The conducting forum begins with the usual succinct introductions, participants offering their names and dossiers in the form of wherever they are from. All the music Ivies are represented by the time they get to me and my humble introduction.

"I'm Lindsey Williams, and I teach at Valley Free Academy."

I am met with the room's blank staring silence. I expect no one to know this little town—most don't even know the small city it's near—so I am not surprised. The others have traveled far, some across oceans, to meet the man who changed the landscape for bands worldwide. In the classical music world, the orchestra and the opera hold the largest repertoire of our greatest composers. Beethoven didn't write for band. But that wasn't going to stop Mr. Battisti. He commissioned works from the greatest contemporary composers and built an oasis of wind band repertoire in our world of orchestral prowess.

I'm hoping we'll move on quickly from my small-town hailing when a voice breaks the quiet: "You're from The Valley?" Mr. Battisti exclaims.

I nod, wondering why my little town is of any significance as he addresses the group, bright-eyed.

"I student-taught in The Valley in 1953!"

We start the next morning with an intense score study session, and in the afternoon we each take turns leading a nonet of winds through Gounod's "Petite Symphonie." The clinicians are hard on every conductor, pressing them to defend their musical decisions with motions that make sense. I am nervous but encouraged, because most of the professors' comments are ones Mr. F has already worked me through. As my turn approaches, I set up my phone to record my session.

"Williams," Professor Battisti calls out, and I walk to the front of the room.

"The Scherzo, please," I tell the players. I lift my hands, taking what feels like the biggest risk of my professional life, and do what Mr. F taught me—will myself to look at my players and not the notes before me.

With no page to bind me, the composer's music spins before my eyes, the dots and dashes of their Morse code cutting across time. I feel the artist's original intention, a water table of revelation beneath my feet, and it wells from me, entering a new existence through the end of my baton, becoming the palette from which my players will paint. My hands show what someone else's sound should feel like, and there I become a conductor.

My preparations are well-received all week, and I feel myself grow exponentially in every session, just like my students do at All-State. By the end of the clinic, I know I am on the right path, and I can't wait to bring back all I've learned to try with my students. I'm finally all in.

The last session concludes with Mr. Battisti speaking from the prepared readings we've been assigned, which are mostly from books I already had memorized. His passion is contagious. Everyone feels like I do when we're around him—utterly inspired. Never has our work seemed more compelling than when he describes it.

"Questions?" he asks as he approaches the end of his session. Hands shoot up.

"How long does it take to make a program yours?" asks one participant.

"Fifteen years," Mr. Battisti replies without a moment's hesitation.

A murmur runs through the room. His answer surprises me too, and the participant who asked it prods a little more.

"I've often heard people say four years, since that's how long it takes for students who had the old teacher to graduate from high school or college programs. Why do you say it takes fifteen?"

"It just does," he says definitively. "People," he continues addressing us all, "making music is risky business. It takes time, a great deal of time, for your communities to risk something real with you. They've got to see you risk what you have for them, every time you take the podium. This is why you've got to stay inspired. Why you must read poetry. Walk in nature. Do absolutely everything to stay curious, no matter what the risk." And then he recites words I've read daily for years.

> *"If you can make one heap of all your winnings*
> *And risk it on one turn of pitch-and-toss..."*

The room is full of his silence and his aura as we wait for the rest. But I cannot stop myself from finishing the line from the Kipling poem that already means so much to me.

"And lose, and start again at your beginnings," I say, and he turns to me.

"And never breathe a word about your loss," I finish.

"Exactly!" he replies in delight.

I tell these and other anecdotes to Mr. F. across the table at our favorite restaurant. The only payment he will take for our lessons is a good meal out, where we inevitably talk shop the entire time. I tell him how the symposium's intense score study sessions confirmed his preparations for me, and he nods in satisfaction. I recount moments when I had not only the answers to intimidating questions—acquired in my hours spent adoring tidy lines of typeface text—but the confidence to then convey them to a room full of strangers. Mostly he smiles and nods over the comfort of his crossed arms as we wait for our food.

"You are lucky," he cautions after the story about the poem, which he sees as having more to do with happenstance than hard work.

He is right. I am lucky, but not in the way he thinks.

It's not luck to finish the phrases ignited by a poetic professor, because it's not luck to know obscure lines of verse when you read them every day. It's something else. But I accept my good fortune, however she chooses to smile upon me, and I gleam back at her familiar fleeting face.

Luck, as I see it, is to land in the middle of nowhere and meet one you are meant to meet. The rest is learned. Mr. F's "luck" arrived with me in the big city, where I should have struggled in a sea of so much talent, but swam instead, with the wisdom he strengthened in me. I know now I was right to weather his rough words, because he always knew what I needed to do. And he made my middle of nowhere the center of our universe.

He beams more with every record I report, and I don't know if it's Mr. Battisti's beginning on our stage that is so special to him, or the fact that I found it. I feel the table turning between us, as I teach my own teacher about this connection, which we could have discovered no other way. This is the real gift I give him today for all the hours he has sunk into my slow-growing skill.

Our conversations shift to the music we are planning for the fall. He shares tunes and themes he has planned for his Big University Band, and I for the band that will always be ours. We swap songs like trading cards, and I jot down his ideas for me on my phone.

"The students are begging me to do 'Danzas Cubanas,'" I say.

"Well, you've certainly got the percussionists to do it."

I make a note to myself below my list of favorite pieces.

"Oh, have you heard 'Danzon No. 2'?" I ask him. He smiles. Of course he has.

"You're not planning on programming *that* are you?" he asks, suddenly a little concerned about my sanity.

"Oh, no! It's *way* too hard for us. But it's my favorite piece," I add.

Soon I've remembered something else from my exit interview with Mr. Battisti that I wanted to share. "When you go home," Mr. Battisti told me, "fly in wider circles." When I've recounted this to Mr. F, he shifts in his seat.

"Ya know," he says, "I'm scheduled to present a clinic at this year's conference called *Coaching the Big Band Rhythm Section*. I'm wondering if Jazz I might want to serve as a live demonstration band."

"Yes!" I reply without hesitation, understanding the opportunity he's handing me: a chance to stand alongside him, my mentor, more equal than ever before.

Another risk.

Another gift.

As we make more plans over our bursting burgers, I can taste how sweet he has made his retirement. It is not the end I thought it would be, but a place for his most important possibilities.

We call in Jazz I for extra rehearsals, warming up with the circle of fifths and sharpening every detail for his bi-weekly visits. Mr. F stands in front of the jazz band with me—something we never got to do while he worked at the Academy. He coaches the rhythm section and I the horns, and the fall concert is like none we have ever led.

Practically perfect, my pre-K clan, now juniors, command

the stage for all to see. I feel their success like it's my own, and on the car ride home I let myself imagine the fantastic senior year they will have. What a grand finale to our thirteen years of hard work. I will no longer wonder what I can accomplish when they stand before me as seniors after sharing every step. I'll finally own my own accolades, knowing I have taught them all that they know. I can almost taste the victory of this validation, almost touch its finish-line proof that I have finally become good at this.

And after a fall of wonderful concerts, our voyage to the All-State December Conference is upon us. Parents pack the buses, and every leg of our journey unfolds in ease. Chaperones chat and students play games, while the driver hums us happily forward.

On arrival, the setup is smooth, and miles away from the Valley, we are at home with each other. Matthew meets us there because he has been accepted into the All-State Band, and so does Arthur who is filling in on bass trombone. After a warmup and quick break, the band takes their place as our audience of educators files in.

"Thank you for choosing this session today," Mr. F begins. "I'd like to welcome Mrs. Williams, Director of Bands at Valley Free Academy, and their Jazz I ensemble. We are going to get started with some warmups you can use with your bands when you get back to school."

My students are nervous, but Mr. F has placed this warmup demonstration not just for the audience, but for us too. By the end of our Circle of Fifths demonstration, our jitters are all out and we move on to finer topics. Mr. F and I work easily off each other, polished from our shared time together. He narrates and we demonstrate. Finally, the band wraps up the session with a driving arrangement of "Birdland."

Our energy is infectious, and our audience is appreciative.

After the final hit, they are on their feet in ovation.

My students' parents come forward to congratulate their kids and help pack up. Educators with more questions converse with Mr. F, hanging on his every word. He is even more respected than I realized. Miss Garnet—who has come to our clinic after presenting one herself—greets our students with hug after hug, and I find Matthew before he heads back to his next All-State rehearsal.

"How is everything going?" I ask.

"Great," he replies. "But it will be even better next year, when James and Julian can be here too."

"Yes," I agree with a smile.

He heads off, and I return to the next task of the trip. Once we are packed up, the parents present us with a banquet of pizza and, hearts and bellies full, we head home like heroes. After we unload at school, I open my desk drawer and tuck the program from our session into my manila file.

The risk was worth it. When Mr. F announced me as, "Director of Bands at Valley Free Academy," it finally felt true.

The year continues with our modern band's packed gig at a local pizzeria. Music memorized, Julian and his friends dance like rock stars between tables and slices of the town's best pie. Even the bartender remarks that he has never heard the band sound so good. I feel it too, that well of inspiration surging beneath their feet. A few days later, I squeeze photos of the night into my file, which is nearly bursting now, but I do not let myself look through it, not wanting to jinx our success. Our work is finally paying off, and there is no reason we can see that will keep next year from being even better.

YEAR THIRTEEN

"And lose, and start again at your beginnings
And never breathe a word about your loss;"

~Rudyard Kipling

A Day Like Any Other

IN JANUARY, WE INVITE several retired directors to lead workshops on each instrument. Always within earshot, I learn countless lessons aired by these experienced guests. Mr. F is one of them, of course, and we fall into the familiar, lunching in our usual way. In February, never missing a musical, he gives me conducting tips from his drum set after every run-through. Some are simple. All are significant. And although it isn't exactly like old times, it's its own kind of kinship, freed from the currents of obligation.

This indefinable emulsion of friendship and mentorship fills our sails and—attempting to stay one step ahead of my students' approaching ennui—I invite Mr. F to come coach our concert band in preparation for spring performances. Together we tackle winter's icy monotony and a classic air he recommended last summer. But despite our enthusiasm for maudlin music, March's long weekend tantalizes our students from the clock in the corner. They want nothing more than a break from school's cruel repetition.

"Yes, you've got the notes, but where's the meaning?" he prods after their halfhearted rendition of a tune they think they already know.

To their uncomfortable silence he says, "Repeat after me."

Then he speaks the rhythm of their ambiguous phrase with an arc of calculated emphasis. They echo it back reluctantly from their seats. He is not convinced.

"No. Engage your air." He models it, rhythmically hissing the phrase again. They repeat it, less breathless, more attentive this time, but it isn't enough.

"Again," he insists, pressing them to improve through several more attempts. Barely satisfied, he gusts forward.

"Now play it that way."

And they do.

"Now do that in the next section," he continues.

The director has spoken, and his atmosphere is everywhere when I interrupt.

"Wait," I say pointing to a tricky series of entrances. "How should I show them this?"

Mr. F bends for a moment over the score, and I feel the room shrink, soundless. I suppose I could have waited to ask. But it felt too important. So, fully undefended I stand there, being seen as his student by my own for the first and last time.

"Show them this instead," he dictates, pointing to a breath a beat before. The students do not see our strategy, only that we converse comfortably, a gnomon clocking our time together over ticking bar lines.

As I take the baton, he rolls his own shoulders back, his subtle reminder for me to bring the baton and the band to me. I start small, activating the air in my upbeat and releasing the first phrase smaller still. They feel the intentions of each approaching ictus with the one in my hand.

Then I take the opportunity he indicated, a sliver of space filled with collective breath—something we will not experience for months to come. I expand back with their crescendo, riding their air instead of reaching for it. Their sound increases, more immense with each entrance, and they know it's better because I listened to him. Wind-roiled, they ride it too, a hidden curriculum with unexpected outcomes.

That day, our whole world is within those walls. A train of three generations aimed at the same goal. After rehearsal, students linger, until they must finally answer the aching call for coveted cafeteria chicken nuggets. It is a day like any other. Ordinary as air. I take no photo for the box I have yet to make. But I'll always remember it because it is the last time we ever do this. I replay it in my mind over the empty months that follow. Our students get the break they wished for from winds they never wanted.

We don't return to school on the Monday after our long weekend, or for many Mondays to come, because what wafts around us is suddenly sick. A strange illness has made its way across the sea, threatening the life in our lungs and infecting our freedom. Our imagined futures of grand finales and successful senior years are replaced with viral fears. The closeness we shared is the very thing that sickens, and therefore must separate us.

Sadly, it seems my most excellent thirteenth year is unlucky after all.

One-Lady Band

WHEN SCHOOL IS CANCELLED for the first week, it catches me by surprise. When school is cancelled until the end of April, I start doing online lessons and helping my own children through virtual first and third grade. When school is cancelled through the end of the year, I lie awake at night questioning my life choices to be a band director.

The news fills with stories of choirs being super-spreaders of this virus that remains dormant in some while killing others. Making music together is now feared and prohibited. Angry tears soak my pillow.

I finally commit to this band director thing, taking all these risks, and now what? What if the world really is different after this? What will I do? I don't even know who I am if I'm not a music teacher.

I roll over.

This is so unfair! First the flood; now this. My poor pre-K class. I cannot let this be how our story ends.

It is impossible to find any perspective in my soggy pillow, so I get up and head downstairs. Pacing the living room, I remember missing them during my maternity leave, and the year they moved on to high school without me. Now here we are, missing precious time again, right when we should be at the glorious finale we've worked so hard for.

And where is my precious box when I need it most? I never took the time to make one, so it's still just a flimsy file sitting at school—a place I am not even allowed to visit. I feel quarantined from my own story, with no connection, no perspective, and certainly no grand climactic ending.

To make matters worse, my dad must go in for his heart checkups at Mount Sinai alone, and my own immediate family is struggling like everyone else's. The extra time with them is the only gem of this situation. Everyone I know is afraid—afraid they will lose their job, their health, their family members, or their lives.

I continue my pacing.

I need perspective, my upperclassmen need closure, we all need connection, and I know it. The question is, *How do we get it?*

I lean my head on the built-in bookshelf by my fireplace. Mr. Battisti's books sit beside my own high school yearbook and an eclectic smattering of *Harry Potter* and poetry volumes. I open my senior yearbook, indulging my pity party for the seniors who are not getting theirs.

It falls right open to a photo of my high school marching band. The page is covered in signatures from nearly every member. The next page is filled with news headlines from that year. The top story is September 11th. I see happiness and hardship from another time, and I have an idea.

"Good morning, folks." I begin our Zoom class in the usual way, hiding my own anxiety from all the households overhearing us. It is May 1st, and teachers everywhere are trying everything, hoping anything but upper respiratory symptoms will go viral. While we stumble, student engagement plummets. Our Zoom classrooms are dark. Students leave their cameras off and type one-word answers to my questions in the chat to appease my nagging. Nothing feels real, or worth it, so I have nothing to lose by trying...

"Today we are going to start a new project," I announce and click the next slide. "Instead of sitting here for class, I need you to go on a hunt." There is no threat of being interrupted online, so I just keep monologuing. "For today's class, your assignment is to go to your bookshelves or closets or attics or basements, and look for old photos, programs, articles, or anything at all about our band. Email me photos of what you find, and we'll share them as they come in." Grateful for the break, they sign off and I am left wondering if they are really doing this or just lying in their beds.

They return for our next class with items they have found and take turns sharing these with the group. One camera at a time flicks on and it feels like show-and-tell. I know at least one student at a time is engaged, and I am enjoying the change of pace as well. Rose has found an article from the 1950s that zooms us to an era of early morning drum and bugle corps rehearsals.

"Did you know we had an all-girls drum and bugle corps?" she asks me.

"I had no idea," I admit.

Leah flicks on her screen. "Hey, I know this is crazy, but my grandma was in the group. She's sitting right here, if you want her to tell us about it."

"Sure," I say. "Put the expert on!"

Leah's grandma is a breath of fresh air. She has us in stitches, laughing over her tales of oppressively hot wool marching-band uniforms and travel fiascos. I post about our project on social media and retired directors scan us past programs. Slowly, we piece together a story—one of stability punctuated by the disruptions of war and recession.

Unable to travel in our time, we travel through it instead, searching our yearbooks for the perspective we lack. By the end of the school year, we've learned that our director in 1900 was the prolific composer Philip Paul Bliss, and our director from 1920 to 1942, Frank Tei, led the band in live radio broadcasts every Sunday. Our hearts break for the band of 1943 as we learn director after director was drafted, and one extraordinary woman, Evelyn Wells, taught chorus, orchestra, and band until the war was over. But it is the photo from 1946—filled with happy faces and a huge band huddled around the very same bass drum I know from my room before the flood—that reassures us we will recover too.

One story leads to another, and we find ourselves inviting Mr. Battisti to a June Zoom class for an interview.

"What did you learn while student-teaching here?" James asks.

Mr. Battisti's reply is immediate. "I learned to appreciate all the experiences I had and everyone who provided them."

"And where did you grow up?" Matthew chimes in with the next question.

"Well, right up the road from you all, actually. In a small town few people have heard of." I am surprised to learn this too.

"Do you think that influenced you?" Matthew prods.

"Most certainly," Mr. Battisti answers. "Being surrounded by such natural beauty—the forests, the rivers, lakes, and gorges—was a very inspiring way to grow up."

The band is just as enamored with him as the summer conducting fellows, and they ask him question after question until our hour is up.

"Do you have any last pieces of advice for us?" Ashton asks, wrapping up our session.

Mr. Battisti waves a finger at the camera. "Strive to give the best you can to all your endeavors. And commission!"

"Commission?" I can see some of my students are confused. They haven't played a commissioned piece since their fifth-grade year.

"Yes, ask a composer to write a new piece for us," I clarify, a bit embarrassed that I've let them forget. "Where should we start?" I ask back.

"With Dana Wilson, of course!" Mr. Battisti replies. "He was a composition professor at the college right up the road from you and still lives close by."

All summer our administration makes difficult calls on scheduling for the coming year, and we learn that core classes will meet partially in-person, while special-area classes— music included—will remain virtual all year long. This decision hits our elementary and middle school music programs hardest, and I see how much it drains Miss Garnet. Most of my band continues to meet online at 9:00 a.m. before the bus runs. Only a few very small-group classes of my pre-K seniors are allowed to attend in-person during the day. I am thankful to be back in my band room with a few of them, even though we still can't have rehearsals. I rack my brain for any way to make this year special for them. The only idea I have is Mr. Battisti's commission, so I follow it.

One of my small in-person classes has only Rose, Ashton, and the twins in it. They naturally become my advisory council for the project, and together we draft a letter to Dr. Dana Wilson with our favorite historical find yet: the story of a one-lady band who performed in the Valley in the early 1900s. We ask him to write a piece based on her manuscripts to honor Mr. Battisti's 90th birthday. As soon as he hears Mr. B's name, he's in.

He gives us a great price, but it's still thousands more than we have. We need to fundraise more than I have experience with, and I am truly stressed by this part of the project. Rose's class and I make call after call searching for community collaborators, but most inquiries go unanswered. Some people in our rural area have never heard of a commission and are wary of our requests, especially during quarantine. Getting this off the ground is proving far more difficult than I imagined.

I drive home frustrated, traffic grinding to a halt near the fireman's fountain as everyone from the school heads to the highway after work. Stuck between two red traffic lights, I turn toward the statue on my left. The Fire Department has now restored it to all its former glory. He has been perfectly repainted, and water flows from his fountain.

Right! I think. *Our Fire Department restored the fountain.* I can still smell the amazing chicken barbecues they hosted to raise money for it. *Maybe they can help.* Ashton and I make the call as soon as we get to school the next day.

"So do you think you could help us?" Ashton asks after explaining everything.

"We would love to!" the Fire Captain replies.

She smiles, and Rose and I breathe our first sigh of masked relief.

Most band members remain distanced through January, practicing at home and becoming composers and arts advocates from afar. Everything extra remains cancelled, including Julian's private trombone lessons, which he really needs to prepare for his college auditions.

"I know it's not the same, but I'd be happy to give him private lessons if you are comfortable with it," I offer his mother.

"Oh, of course. I'll meet you at the church, and you can do spaced-out lessons in the sanctuary." She waits in the social hall while we fill the church with the only live music I've heard in months. We meet there on Wednesdays after school and practice till the sun shrinks from the stained glass, and we are left playing across the pews in the dark. The lessons never seem long enough, and we spend most of the winter making Julian's college audition recordings.

One blustery evening, Mr. F and I catch up over the phone. I tell him about my lessons with Julian and our band's commission. He tells me he is just as busy trying to plan virtual projects and distanced concerts with his University band. We trade ideas, just like always. He is excited about lots of new composers and pieces. I am surprised that he seems unfazed by all this.

"So many folks I know are worried about the arts and education, but you don't seem to be. Are you?" I ask, trying to hide my own doubts.

"Not at all," he says. "This will pass. We will always need good music and good teachers." His voice sounds so certain over the phone, like he speaks only truths, and it emboldens my own convictions.

Meanwhile, my small in-person classes spend weeks planning a deliciously distanced chicken barbecue. On the day of the fundraiser, Rose, Ashton, and Saoirse scoop beans six feet apart, while my Three Musketeers and Rhyse run orders to the cars like masked barbecue bandits. Dan and the parents keep the traffic and the cashbox flowing, and we end the day smelling of barbecue and sweaty success.

Our anticipation increases as the delivery of the first draft approaches. Then one February morning, a simple email titled "New Piece!" arrives in my inbox. My heart pounds as I read it over. After a few minor revisions, we send the next draft to Mr. B, and within the hour, I answer my phone to his exclamation.

"I love it! It's exciting, new, and fresh! When's the premiere? I want to be there."

I share the score with the students and play its basic ideas for them over Zoom, asking what they think. Suddenly, blank cameras flicker on, and the chat streams a waterfall of comments. Excitement explodes across unstable internet connections, obliterating the Zoom-induced epidemic of enervation and indifference.

They know this is no exercise. We have a job to do.

This is our story. This is our art.

All spring they practice their parts, and many students I haven't seen all year come in, one at a time, to record their tracks in the band room. We piece it all together, and in June we watch our virtual premiere with friends and family over Zoom. Mr. F is among them.

When the piece concludes, I say, "Happy Birthday!" and Mr. B. claps his hands together, saying, "That's what good music does!"

He leans all ninety of his years close to his screen, almost whispering now.

"You must pursue things you are passionate about. Not things that will get you something, but things you do because you just have to. Stay curious and find out what that means."

His words settle across our screens, and before I can segue, an unexpected voice joins the conversation.

"I know what it means," a quiet sophomore pipes up from her usually silent square. "This year...well, honestly, every year..." She shrugs. "It's been so easy to feel separated from everyone. It's felt like there is no goal worth working for. But..." She stammers slightly. "But doing this has connected what I thought we couldn't. It made me feel something when I was numb, and I'm proud I hauled myself out of bed and was part of it."

I am stunned by her vulnerability. Then Rose chimes in.

"Yes, doing this has focused me on making something positive, instead of everything else."

The twins, Violet and Valerie, nod from their shared Zoom square.

Ashton unmutes and adds, "It made me forget what's happening and remember what's real. It showed me why we make music, even if we had to do it behind these screens, or six feet apart with masks."

More exaggerated Zoom nods flow across my screen, and Julian concludes, "Funny what we had to lose to realize what we wanted."

In all our years together, they have never said so much. It is here—without a single accolade—that my students learn the true value of our art, I learn the value of teaching, and we all learn the value of our time together. We didn't do all this to be right or worthy, we did it to encourage each other.

After the class is over, I print a copy of the score. It too joins the file in my right-hand drawer. I know this is our finale, but it doesn't feel final. It is the end of their time here, but not mine. There is still something I need to do.

Later that week, my Three Musketeers, Rose, Ashton, and I travel down the road to our local radio station, WTVW, for an early-morning interview and FM premiere of our piece. We sit in swivel chairs and answer interview questions into microphones until the announcer Dave says, "What a wonderful project. Let's hear the tune!"

With one little click, just as our 1920s director Frank Tei did, we are broadcasting our band on the radio waves. As our piece plays, I imagine Frank's pride, knowing we told his story with our own, and I see my students smiling because we did it with a song.

After our radio show, in Covid-19's suspended cadence, we meander along the river Where the Valley Widens. We share stories from every grade, 14 years in all, but it doesn't make their leaving any easier. I feel the stone of Sisyphus weighing me down once more.

We amble past the restored fireman statue and admire his fresh paint, shining as bright as the lantern he holds by his side. We sit on the newly installed benches, and my students tell me their future plans. Julian's lessons in the sanctuary have resulted in his acceptance to music school. Rose is enlisting. They are all off to great adventures. Our grand finale resolves its final chord quietly, with the statue standing over our stories, an inland lighthouse with fountains flowing at his feet and a heron overhead.

"It's done," I say when we reach the school. "We did it."

We all hug, but we do not cry. Then I watch them walk to their cars and move on, while I try not to feel left behind.

"Hey," I hear Julian ask the others on the way. "Wanna grab a bite at the Skylark Diner?"

"Of course," James replies.

"It's our post-concert tradition," confirms Matthew.

"Meet ya there," say Rose and Ashton in unison.

I didn't know they had post-concert traditions, but I am not surprised. There is much about my experience they don't know either. Their banter continues as they close their car doors and zoom off to enjoy Reubens, malted milkshakes, and hopefully, a lifetime of friendship beyond the band room.

I head for my own silver sedan, and though a big part of me wants to go with them, I finally know what I need to do. I need to go get that box.

Con Brio
Years 14 – 18

"...Joy moves from unmarked box to unmarked box,
from cell to cell. As rainwater, down into a flowerbed.
As roses, up from the ground...
It hides within these,
till one day it cracks them open."

~Rumi

YEAR FOURTEEN

"If you can force your heart and nerve and sinew
To serve your turn long after they are gone,"

~Rudyard Kipling

The Box

THROUGH QUARANTINE'S EMPTINESS I've continued to enjoy periodic visits to the *Old, Odd, and Unique* antique shop. I spend pandemic summers the same way I spent my first one: rescuing and fixing the stray instruments I find there. Some require a technician's expertise but many I restore with borrowed parts from instruments the professionals deemed "beyond repair." Re-pairing parts of two broken instruments often results in one funtional one and gives me a new understanding of the word.

After an entire pandemic of overhauls—and the instrument donation drives of one Gold Award earning Girl Scout—our shelves are full and our district can now supply nearly every student with an instrument free of charge. Lonnie now greets me by name and cashes me out at cost. He knows what I'm doing. He's doing it too.

An excited little bell always announces our arrival at his store with a pleasing triplet jingle. His kind blue eyes dart up at the sound, greeting us from behind his mop of dusty gray-brown hair and silver-rimmed glasses. Even the masks of Covid-19 can't dampen his smile. He is always ready with instruments for me and knick-knacks for my children, who are perpetually on the hunt for treasures of their own.

During my last visit, from behind his desk, he unveiled the pieces of an antique wooden flute. The serial number dated it to 1890 or earlier, and my inspection revealed not a single crack in this caseless castaway. I bought it, restored it, and purchased a leather knife roll for its case. Now I play Irish tunes on it in our evening living room *seisiúns* with Saoirse on fiddle, Rhyse on cajon, and Dan on guitar. I see it as a gift from the cosmos, to receive back what I had given, to be paid in kind for my work.

"How ya doing there, Williams crew?" Lonnie greets us today as the bell announces our arrival.

"Great, Lonnie! Got any instruments for me?"

"Nothing new since last time, but I've got a few things for the kiddos."

Dan and the kids follow him up to the glass counter, ogling a shark tooth and the pocket watches he has there. While my family upholds our customary instrument-trinket custom, I make my usual storewide circumambulation. It leads me to a table in the back where I know a flat wooden silverware box usually sits under a layer of dust. I've seen it before, snuggled in with the cigar boxes. It's been here a long time, and although it's caught my eye many times, I've always been too laden with instruments to add it to my purchases. I can't believe someone else hasn't bought it by now.

It's beautiful in its simplicity, stained dark, with a single black handle on the lid. I open it. Its decrepit troughs stand empty, its valuable silver sold off long ago. Its lining is coming undone at the seams, and its little nameplate hangs cockeyed by a single pin—the other one long lost, I am sure. I guess that's why it's still here. It looks good from the outside, but the inside needs some serious work. I carry it to the counter.

"Not your usual fare, I see," Lonnie comments with a raised white eyebrow.

"Yes. It's for a project I've been thinking about for a while now. I finally have the time to do it," I say.

"Sounds important," he says.

"Yeah, I guess it is."

We check out with the day's catch of an empty box and the ever-coveted children's baubles. My husband even springs for the shark tooth, so the kids are on cloud nine. Then my family and I pile into the car and drive to my childhood home. My dad is recovering from his recent pacemaker implant, so we chat with him, masked and distanced on the porch, while my mother, the seamstress, gathers everything we need.

She knows how to mend anything. Every inch of her house proves this. It is filled with classic furniture she has reupholstered and curtains she has tailored to the oversized windows of her turn-of-the-century home. I show her the box. She already knows what it's for and we commence with the demolition, removing its dilapidated trays, frayed lining, and crusty bits of glue. Dan and my dad talk while Saoirse and Rhyse try to help us. When the summer heat melts their resolve, they sneak off to the basement freezer in search of their favorite purple popsicles and my mother goes off to her sewing room again to hunt for a remnant of better upholstery.

While I wait for her to return, I reflect on the box and its complete emptiness. Time, neglect, and a bit of our hard work have nearly ruined this fine piece. But Lonnie, my mom, and I know it is simply done being a silverware box. That part of its story is over. It has a new purpose now.

That afternoon we repair and shine its hinges and brass nameplate, refinish its wood, and reline it with a bit of pink linen. I place the nameplate from the original box on the fabric

my mother lined it with. Its words are heavy in my hand and
on my tongue.

Marjory B. Hinman
– 1949 –

"Who is she?" we wonder. I grab my phone, and a quick
internet search yields our answer.

"She lived from 1927 to 2014 in the outskirts of our area," I
paraphrase from the web. "She was the founder and president
of several local historical societies. She worked for more than
thirty years in schools, libraries, and museums while writing
eleven books on the history of this place she called home."

My mom looks at me.

"It seems fitting that a box that once held her treasures
now holds yours," she says.

"I like that," I say, as I close the box.

"Me too," she says.

As the sun sits low in the sky, my family and I sit back to
admire the handiwork of this sweltering quarantine day before
setting off for dinner. They have all helped me make this
beautiful box, and it is just what I needed.

When I return home, I take the simple manila file folder I
have been using all these years and quickly transfer its
contents to the box without looking. Today is not the day I
don't want to be a teacher anymore, as Mr. O'Dell said so many
years ago. Today is not the day to review my collection. Today
is about the box I've avoided making for so long. Finally, I've
done it. I've made something sacred from the driftwood that
was left to me. Step One of my assignment is complete.

It only took me fourteen years, but I finally have my box.

Letters

IN QUARANTINE'S SANCTUARY of time and space, I read like I do in summer—everything I can get my hands on. I read young adult series to know the stories that inspire my students. I read picture books in voices to my children. I read fantasy, fiction, and poetry to feel the boundless imagination of our world. I also read about teaching and directing, about great composers and their music. These books have been some of my greatest teachers, telling me what I wasn't ready to hear in real life. Showing me, from the safety of my armchair, the risks worth taking and how to live in *The Art of Possibility*.

In a book named just that, in the year I took over Jazz II, I found an interesting assignment. Students write a letter in past tense, dated the last day of their impending school year, addressed to their teacher or themselves, describing how they earned their "A" that year. I have tried this experiment in classes over the years, and often students would just provide a straightforward answer that matched the pre-written comments on their report cards. While I am tidying up the band room for its annual summer cleaning, I find a pile of them in a manila envelope labeled "A Papers." I roll my chair up to the desk and open the folder over my computer keyboard.

June 2018

Dear Mrs. Williams,

I deserve an A because my name starts with an A :) Also, I practiced my music outside of class. I was always prepared and I didn't disrupt everyone. I was on time to concerts and I did a plethora of extra activities outside of school.

Signed,

Your "A" Student, Ashton

Others answered like this:

June 2019

Dear Mrs. Williams,

I deserve an A because I am better than James. So since James is getting an A, and I am better, it would make sense if I also received an A. (Also you're the best and I try to play the music right.)

Thomas

And this:

June 2019

Mrs. Williams,

I deserve an A because I always play my part really good and this part of my day is the best and I love being here making music with great people. Also, I am better than Thomas so don't listen to him.

James

I tuck these in my bag, knowing they will all end up in my box, each for their own endearing reason. Then I come across a more recent letter. When I offered this assignment again this year, from behind the mask of half-lived hybrid education, I received this one from one of my pre-K clan members:

Hi Mrs. Williams,

This isn't exactly the "A Paper" you asked for, but I just wanted to thank you for calling me my new name today, instead of Rose. It is the happiest I've ever been. I was so scared to make the change, in front of everyone, but when you just called me Ryan, like it was easy, I finally felt comfortable too. I have never been happier, and I just wanted you to know that. It's an "A" I never thought I could earn.

Throughout the years of knowing each other, you saw me for who I was, and you allowed me to be whoever I wanted to be, no matter who I was at the moment. You let me be a flute player and then a trumpet player. You made the band room, the music office, and oddly enough, the band practice closet... (haha), all safe spaces for me. I was able to be myself, in all my forms, while making music throughout all the years of knowing you. The band room will always be a safe space for me, and many other students (and adults) regardless of how long they're there. I thank you endlessly for all you've done,

Ryan

He is right. It is not the paper I asked for. It is something else. It was never meant for my gradebook. It's for my box. I tuck it in my bag with the others to take home.

Then I turn to file a mountain of music recently returned to me from the Finches after a healthy bout of quarantine cleaning. I open a well-loved *Trombone Book 1* to see dates in my handwriting snuggled in the side margins. They are right where I left them thirteen years ago.

I am moving to return the dog-eared book to its place in our library when a single slice of wide-ruled remembrance drifts to the floor in escape.

I pick up the time traveler and enter the mind of Arthur Finch, when he was in fourth grade:

March 2009

Dear Journal,

I don't know why they worry. I love it here. Everyone is so nice. I get letters from school and I play video games all day! They said I can go home soon but that I'll have to take the IV with me to school. I guess no one ever asked them if you can play the trombone with one of these since they didn't have an answer for me but I can't wait to try!

Sincerely,

Arthur

And try he did. I remember how he came to lessons, trombone in one hand, IV pole in the other. He had been so seriously sick, but all he saw around him was joy.

"Welcome back!" I remember saying.

He smiled widely as he prepared his trombone with the help of his band buddies. With just a little extra effort, he was ready to go, and with their backs to winter's gray afternoon sky, I asked, "Are you sure you're okay to play?"

He smiled again at his trombone, saying, "I have medicine."

His buddies didn't hear him over the clamor of their own clinking slides, but I knew he was okay. So we played together against the ever darkening skies and made an old medicine for each other.

His letter is my only one from before the flood and its own kind of "A Paper." I tuck the time traveler in my bag and return the book, along with some others, to its home in our manicured music library.

When I return home that evening with my unexpected "A"

papers, I head to my box, intending to add them to the rest. Instead, I find myself taking out a pen and paper, and as all good teachers do, I complete the assignment myself:

Dear Teacher,

I earned my "A" because I never gave up. When it was the hardest of all, I smiled the most. I've been doing it so long I can't remember when I started. I began earning my "A" many years ago when I listened to your words and you became my teacher when I had none. I continued to earn my "A" because I let you affect me and I have never been the same. I earned my "A" when I learned there is no grade, only the gifts we give each other.

Always,

Your Student

This letter to my teachers and myself is the first one I drop in my box. But I am not done. I take out a clean page and write one more.

Dear Band,

I earned my "A" because every day I walked into rehearsals like you were the All-State Band and I was your guest conductor. I never wanted to miss a chance to do something amazing with you. I could never know what would become of you, so I gave you my best and you made me who I am.
I know this year has been especially hard on music (and humanity) everywhere, but I want you to know that art isn't about perfect people or perfect situations. It's about the broken ones, and the wonder you discover on the dark journeys that break them open to what was once unimaginable.

Since the beginning and always,

Your teacher, Mrs. Williams

I fold it in thirds and drop it in along with the others, mailing all of them to my future self.

And on the day you don't want to be a teacher anymore, you need to open that box and read each one. His words still ring in my ears.

My hand hangs there for a moment. Seeing the "A Papers" makes me want to look at what's inside, but I'm afraid opening it is an admission—that part of me doesn't want to do this anymore. I fear that the box's pile of papers, all from people who have left my dream for another, will not be enough. I fear my life is just a jumble of others' unfinished fantasies, but most of all mine, and I'm not ready to face that yet. There is still something unfinished for me out there in the Valley.

Instead, I admire my box from the outside. Like my band room, I've built it from what my teachers left me, and it holds my students' scattered stories. This box, built from what I love best, is mine by the way I tend it. It protects the words of what has been, and what might be, waiting for my hand to set its stories so they bring out the beauty in each other. It will hold these possibilities for a short and beautiful time, until the day my students discover this box as driftwood along their shores and build their own from the broken bits of what I've left them.

YEAR FIFTEEN

"And so hold on when there is nothing in you
Except the Will which says to them: "Hold on!"

~Rudyard Kipling

Forget Me Not

EVERY YEAR, I PLANT FORGET-ME-NOTS in the flower beds around my house. I have roses stretching two stories high in every color in which they come, but forget-me-nots will always be my favorite.

I also have a folder on my computer called *Forget-Me-Nots.* Inside are other folders for each school year, and in them, files titled with only a name. Julian Finch. James Gladwell. Ashton Brando. Ryan Winters. They are letters of recommendation. I used to write them by request. This year, I write one for Miss Garnet and one for every senior in the band. I need them just as much as they do. Forget-me-nots are for goodbyes.

The year after my pre-K clan's graduation, we come together slowly, first twelve feet apart, then six, growing together like the forget-me-nots in my garden. Finally unmasked, we play alongside each other as Covid-19's Comeback Kids, and what felt like the end reveals, with new blooms, that it wasn't.

Every spring concert, we fill our intermission with our

Senior Recognition ceremony. I used to watch it when I was the elementary director, with an innocent envy of Mr. F, who had known all the students for so long. It felt like it would take an immeasurable amount of time to be standing in his shoes, but now here I am, without the class that has been my shadow for so long. Now every year will be a year of students I have seen since their beginnings. Every year, I will give them away to the world with my letters in their hands and I'll say something between musical sets to make sense of this passing of time and torch.

This year I say:

Seniors, and students of any age, my message to you is this: Stand still. These sudden ends of time should give you pause. So stop. Whatever you do, do not let your life become an afterthought. See what you have made here. If you cannot see it, I will tell you: You have made life more beautiful for those around you. There is nothing more important. It is because of this that you have become important to us. Know this and do not fray into your future undone.

When you are worried, stop and see what is seeking you. Then step forward deliberately. Your music will always be there for you, and so will we. So as you leave us, I say to you, the world is good. Go see it. Go be it. Become engineers, athletes, nurses, writers, teachers, parents. Become a master of whatever you choose. Become a great story or a great song. Become the whole world. Then stand still and see it.

If we had not been halted and quarantined, separated from our own lives, could we have appreciated them so fully?

No matter the year, at the end of April's concert they are never ready to hear these words. "It doesn't feel like the end yet," the seniors always agree.

But it is. It's done.

They spend the next two months—their last two months—detaching. They step away with each awards ceremony, senior skip day, prom, and finally graduation. Every year my fellow teachers complain about their ever-enlarging senioritis and irresponsibility. But something important is happening. With every ball the seniors drop, a surprising new hand reaches out to take it as their own. In their absence, we learn just how much the underclassmen have grown. They are always ready. This is how we take our next step.

We don't miss them because of the talents they take with them or the trail of accomplishments they leave in their wake. We miss their voices. We miss the flavor of our lives when we were with them. And we would miss their stories if they weren't our stories too.

One day after school, Miss Garnet pulls me aside.

"I just wanted to say thanks for that letter you wrote for me. I got the job," she says with a shy smile. We hug and are happy. It's exciting, like she is graduating too. But secretly I wonder what I'm doing here, helping everyone move on except me.

Every year at graduation, the band plays and the valedictorian speaks, and when the seniors process across the stage, I always imagine Mrs. Ferri reading their names on the afternoon announcements one last time. I see their families waiting to pick them up, just as they have done for the past 2,520 days of school. Then the graduates toss their caps, and the band heralds them out, and the train of people who have left just gets longer and longer.

Goodbye

MOTIVATED BY THE DESIRE to see even just a few of our graduates again—and by some other unknown force—I start a summer alumni band. To fill all our seats, we partner with the neighboring district that hosted us during the flood. The collaboration feels like a coincidence, but I know it's not. It's only right that we should finally share some success after all we have weathered.

I work relentlessly to get it off the ground in time for summer, and the first person to arrive to pick up his music is Mr. F. I hand him his folder, but instead of leaving, he stays, and together we greet alumni as long-lost family. Some are my Covid-19 kids, but even more are his students, long back from college with children of their own. White-haired community members who predate even Mr. F point to cases on our shelves that were once theirs and thank us for getting the band back together again.

At one point, the line reaches out the door with people waiting, not so much for their music, but for a chance to say just one sentence to the walking legend, Mr. F. It feels like a receiving line without the somber sentiments. When the last of them have left, he turns to me.

"Well, that was fun!" His eyes are alight with the same joy I saw during his "Sleigh Ride" sendoff. Then he pivots.

"Hey," he says, pulling a paper from the brown satchel at his side, "what do you think of these concert programs?"

I take the paper to see a year's worth of plans for his Big University Band. Program after program is filled with his favorites and mine. Many of the pieces are ones I have recently prepared for our alumni concerts. One program in particular—one he knows I would love beyond all logic—stands out to me.

"Danzas and Danzon! On the same concert! These programs are amazing," I say, appreciating how he set each piece to bring out the excellence of the others. "I would love to conduct these," I add, knowing that occasionally, he lets me cover for him when he's away. I'd never be able to play "Danzon No. 2" with my high schoolers, and I pine to try my hand at these masterworks with a band that can ignite all the life in them. What a gift it would be to rehearse the collegiates on it just once.

"Why don't you keep that," he says. It is not a question and although a part of me wonders why, I don't think much of it.

"Actually, I need to borrow a few pieces from the Academy's library for this year's programs." He points to the page. "I've marked them there."

I pull the last piece as the sun sets, brindling the incoming rain clouds outside our wall of windows. As we walk out the door, his voice shifts.

"I hear you have some new hires."

"Yes, two of them," I confirm. "The new choral teacher is already doing great, but we just finalized the new band director. We had initially chosen someone else with lots of experience, but they declined, so we've got a green one."

We take cover in the alcove outside the band room door as the first raindrops burst like water balloons at our feet.

"I know." His reply is stern. "It seems fate makes the choices you cannot." He tips his chin down at me. "Always pick the one with promise, even if they don't know it yet." He holds his silent stare before stating, "*You* must teach them the rest." His words sink in my stomach. I do not believe in my own untested abilities to teach another adult, but I know to listen to him now. Finally easing off, he adds, "You are lucky."

"I know," I say, admitting to myself that I had ignored something significant in her interview.

"This is the next step, not just for her, but for you too."

His tone is as certain as the rain rolling in around us.

"Ya know," he continues, "your next student teacher did very well in his junior placement with me." He looks at the tree line and says softly, "You're getting a good one."

I can tell this matters to him, that he wants us to have each other for some important reason. I know he is giving me my next round of assignments in our never-ending game, so of course I take them like the gifts they are. I know no other way. Then we talk of repertoire in the rain and only at nature's windy insistence do we part to plant each other's ideas in the time that remains.

We enjoy the newness of our alumni band. Mr. F conducts a whimsical summer "Sleigh Ride" to the delight of our audience, and we conclude our season with a barbecue and jazz concert back outside our band room. Mr. F and I split leading the last concert, taking turns entertaining the crowd, along with my own kids, who dance and play in the open field. When Mr. F isn't conducting, James makes space for him at the drum kit, ever in awe of his teacher. I see the same look of pride cross Mr. F's face when he hears James's fills and setups. The weather is fair, and we all do well, and the audience adores it. While everyone is congratulating each other and cleaning up stands and salt potatoes, Mr. F pulls me aside.

"I need to talk to you," he mumbles under his breath.

My heart stops a little, wondering if I am to receive his usual unfiltered feedback on my general oversights or mismanagement of the rhythm section. To my initial relief, it is not that.

"I want you to know that I am going in for a procedure you are familiar with."

What?

I search his face. He is not being his usual direct self, and my mind races with his riddle. What am I familiar with? My nephew's cancer? My dad's heart surgeries? These are the only "procedures" that come to mind, and I do not like the sound of either one.

"I go in on Tuesday," he says.

"Well," I stammer, unsure of what to say, "I'm even more glad we did all this then."

As the words leave my mouth, I realize what they unintentionally imply and I catch them in my throat, aghast.

"Well..." I cut myself off, attempting to swim from the sinking feeling we are both battling. "...I'll be thinking about you Tuesday."

I want to hug him. I want to ask him more. To say something that makes it all okay. To assure him I will take care of everything. But we are surrounded by people, and we don't want an audience for this. All we can do is say it slant.

So I look at him the way he taught me to look at my players when it's important, when it's my job to conduct comfort through an unsettling entrance. He meets me the same way, sending it right back.

"I know," he says. It is his mantra. It always has been. He has said it a thousand times to me, with a thousand different meanings, but no other time will hold so much as this.

My family and our band members call me back to direct their clean-up efforts, and we nod goodbye to the smell of baked beans and good old-fashioned chicken barbecue. Over stacked chairs and stands and our students' heads, I watch Mr. F walk to his car, parked in his usual spot right next to mine. He closes the door and drives his big blue van away and I pray, with everything I have, that this good day is not goodbye.

YEAR SIXTEEN

"If you can talk with crowds and keep your virtue,
Or walk with kings -- nor lose the common touch,"

~Rudyard Kipling

The New Hire

I TURN FROM MY DESK as our vibrant new band teacher, Miss Lesperance, enters the high school rehearsal room. I reach my hand out to greet her.

"Lindsey," I say. "Pleased to officially meet you."

"Eliza." She reaches her hand out in return. "The pleasure is mine."

There is something different about her. Something different about today as I prepare to share the same (albeit updated) red binder of curriculum Mr. F gave me at a similar session sixteen years ago. It is Wednesday, 9:00 am precisely. We've both arrived early to our meeting, two strangers now attempting to know each other through the syncopations of small talk.

I learn she has come to the Valley by a road resembling my own. We both attended local, less rural high schools. We both auditioned our way into similar prestigious conservatories in urban centers, and we both made the somewhat surprising decision to return home. After our brief conversation, I can't help but think it is likely her struggles will mimic my own, and perhaps I will not be so out of place helping her after all.

"Okay," I begin. "This is a big job, and you are going to need a few things."

She sits taller as I talk to her.

"This is our curriculum," I say, holding out the big red binder I now know by heart.

She takes it, and it drops in her hand with its heaviness, but she doesn't look daunted. "I hope you like reading," I say in part jest.

"Oh, I do," she says, leafing through the first few pages.

She is perusing the Introduction in earnest when I add, "But that's not all you're going to need."

She stops and looks up, the blue flecks in her glasses catching the light.

"You're going to need a box."

"A box?"

"Yup." I hand her a black photo box with a silver nameplate frame that I ordered last week. She sets the binder on a black band chair beside her and takes the box.

"I waited too long to make mine, and we often don't have the time we think we do, so here is your box. The big things you worry about aren't going to fit in there," I tell her. "This is for all the little things you like. It's for all the letters and photos and handmade cards that students—and parents, and even co-workers—give you. It's for whatever comes your way unexpectedly and encourages you to keep going."

Eliza smiles and opens it. In it sits a black notebook and a black Ticonderoga No. 2 Pencil.

"That's for your story," I say. "Write down what you notice—in pencil in case you need to make changes—because sometimes your box won't hold what you were hoping for. If you want to remember some things, you'll just have to write them down yourself. Then whenever you need to, whenever you're ready, read them."

"Thank you," she says, when we are interrupted by my own mentor's number flashing across my phone.

"It's Mr. F!" I say, alight like my screen. "What a coincidence that he's calling right now. I'm sorry, but I have to take this."

"Of course." She nods with an understanding, almost reverent smile. She knows him from afar, respects him from her years as a star student adjacent to, and occasionally intersecting with, his impressive orbits.

I beam as I answer my phone, remembering that just yesterday I awoke to read an out-of-the-ordinary social media post from him, praising my recently published article on commissioning. I immediately texted him my profuse thanks, but I must have missed him in the minutes before his surgery. Now he's calling. What a relief! Everything must have gone well. Now I can thank him personally and tell him our first mentoring session is under way, just like he wanted.

"Mr. F!" I say joyfully, planning to continue with, "Guess what?"

But I never get to say those words.

Instead I hear, "It's not him."

No.

It is his wife who tells me what I know the second I hear her voice instead of his.

"He didn't make it out of surgery."

He's gone.

I can't think.

I can't speak.

I watch these seconds of my life unfold instead of living them myself.

"I didn't know where to begin," she says, "so I just started calling the people he'd last spoken to or texted. I figured maybe he told you about the surgery, and at least I wouldn't have to explain that part. He was so private, you know. He told almost no one about it."

Eliza shifts uncomfortably in her chair, hearing news not meant for her through the echo in my ears—our first lesson interrupted. I'm not sure what she can hear, but it's clear she knows the moment I do what has happened. So I sit there, between her beautiful beginning and his brutal end, and I share my sorrow with this stranger. Her slender hands, cupped neatly around her box, hold my hope while I listen to his wife recount what she knows but cannot yet believe. I want to take Eliza's hand and tell her it will be okay, tell myself the same thing, but that seems too scary for two strangers, each in their own sets of new shoes.

"The doctors did everything they could," his wife tells me.

"I'm so sorry. What can I do?"

"Maybe let people in the music community and the school know? There are just so many people to tell."

"Yes, of course. I can do that."

"Okay. I'll call back tomorrow to check in."

"Okay. Talk to you tomorrow."

Stunned, I hang up the phone, along with any happiness I had.

I do not cry.

I cannot.

"I should go," Eliza says, and she quickly moves to leave, but I am not ready to be alone with this.

"No," I say. "It's okay. He wanted us to do this. Let's try to."

"Are you sure?" she asks in concerned kindness.

"I'm sure," I say. "It's always better together."

Despite the difficulty, we choose each other and try again. She knows Mr. F's legacy, but I don't know what she knows about me. So far all we have is small talk and sadness. We sit in his room, surrounded by the instruments he tended, reading the words he wrote, and all I can think is how cruel it is that these unliving objects should outlast the life that made them. I want so desperately to continue on the path he planned for us, but she knows I am hiding my hurt from her.

After thirty minutes, my senses return to me, along with a sense of duty.

"I think I have to call a lot of people," I say finally.

"Yeah." She tilts her head to the right with an empathy beyond her years.

I give her a few more materials to help her get started, and I sense her relief in leaving this too-familiar seat by my side. She gathers the binder and the box and the book and heads for the door. As I watch her leave my room—his room—I am heartbroken, not just that I have lost him but that I am losing this time with her too. For an instant, I thought the three of us were destined to share this great, unbreakable lineage, with me right in the middle. I thought he would show me how to help her, but instead I must become the teacher time has taken from me. In the same instant that I lose my mentor, I've become one.

I spend the rest of the day calling his friends—our friends—with the news. He knows so many people. I talk so much, my voice is hoarse. When the last few folks I finally call already know the news, I know I can stop.

It's 5:00 p.m.

Then I realize I have not told any of our students. I can't call them all. I'll write a social media post with his wife tomorrow to make it public. For now, I pick up the phone one last time and call the studious young man who was once just a monkey on his mother's hip.

"Hi, James," I begin. "It's Mrs. Williams. Do you know why I'm calling?" I hold out hope that the news has already reached him and I don't have to deliver this miserable message myself.

"No," he replies. In a world of texts and emails, a call from your teacher is rare and scary. Why would I be calling?

"I'm so sorry to tell you this, but Mr. F passed away unexpectedly during heart surgery early this morning." I've been speaking this now scripted sentence all day, but the severity of its message finally pierces the armor around my heart as I repeat it to our shared student, this important person we have encouraged together for the past sixteen years.

"Oh," he says. "Wow."

"Yeah." I move through it as I have all day. "We'll share more information publicly soon. I just wanted to tell you first."

His silence is so uncomfortable, I just continue.

"I know you meant something to him."

A beat.

"I know," he replies.

We say goodbye and hang up.

It's the shortest conversation I've had all day, but it's the one that breaks the box holding me together. James speaks like him. Distilled and direct, with silence surrounding everything important. Years of lessons have left a living remnant of my mentor in our student, yet he is unaware of what he holds.

I see similar splinters of my teacher in the comments on my social media post the next day, and in the emails that flood my inbox for weeks. I see him in every inch of the band room he built, his handwriting on our scores and his movements in my own baton. Everywhere I look, there he is, living only now in our broken hearts and once-upon-a-times.

Pie on the Lawn

THE WORDS OF MY POSTS AND EMAILS CONTINUE to tell the world of his passing while missing the mark of my own grief. I read them over and over, but I cannot make sense of their syllables. I spend the next month planning a gathering with his family. We call it Pie on the Lawn, at his son's perfect request. Eliza and Mrs. DuBois help me set out chairs in the open field outside the band room. Hundreds of people crowd under the tents set by the same firemen who barbecued chicken for the band and restored the statue in the square.

I greet everyone in shared mourning, making all the space I can for the feelings of Mr. F's family. We resign ourselves to our seats, and I begin the service by playing "Scarborough Fair" with another shared student. A saxophone quartet of his close friends plays prelude music, and his fellow symphony percussionists serenade us on the marimba he worked for years to acquire for his students. I invite others to share a few words, and they do. Some tributes are lighthearted, and others are full of melancholy. We need them all. Then I stand at the same podium we use for our concerts and speak:

It's been said, "Whatever we have done with our lives makes us what we are when we die. And everything, absolutely everything, counts." Before I came to know Mr. F, I would have used these words to fuel my drive for doing something great. From afar, that is how he appeared to me. Great. Accomplished. Everything I feared I'd never become.

But he took care of me, as he took care of everyone here today. He shared advice when we asked for it, and sometimes when we didn't. He shared every wonderful piece of music he found in every possible way he could because he wanted you to feel what he felt when you heard it. He would never tell you what you were in for. He'd just say, "Listen to this," and sit back to watch you discover it. Over one shared meal, in a fervor induced by my own musical discovery, I mentioned how I wanted to tell everyone what I'd found. He turned his head, looked right at me, and said, "But isn't it best to discover it yourself?" He was right. That was the kind of gift he was always giving. Hidden in plain sight.

Hafiz says, "Now is the season to know that everything you do is sacred." Sharing a meal with Mr. F was like this. Honestly, the real reason we will miss him so much is because everything he did felt like this. The deliberate way he conducted. The fierce way he taught us and the loving way he fought for us. The way he said hello. The way he said goodbye. In the end, we will miss him most, not for the things he did, but for who he was, and who we were when we were with him. So let us play "Sleigh Ride" in summer and sow in sadness the beautiful music he would have made.

I step back to let his friends play for him, knowing that honoring another life is the real reason we've honed all these skills. Their melodies coax the emotions that need to come, and I let myself feel them.

Hugs from hundreds of people cannot hold our disbelief. By the end of the day, I don't know if my memories are my own or just a reel of the photos on the picture boards that I revisit repeatedly trying to teach my mind that he is gone. As we near the end, one of our close friends, David, finds me, but all I can manage by this point is a raw, "I just don't know why it hurts so much."

"Because," he replies, "he is a part of you."

He's right. Losing Mr. F is like losing all those parts of myself he had shown me. My friend must know this because he feels it too. He contains one, if not many, of those fragments I thought I'd never see again, those inadvertently adopted pieces that were once Mr. F's ways and words. Together at Pie on the Lawn, we live like he would have, sharing pieces of his pie, music, and memory so he can be whole in our lives one more time. I turn to my friend, and we embrace each other's pain as our own.

When I get home, I climb my creaky old staircase in procession to my box. I gently slide the funeral program in and close the top without looking. It lands without a sound, padded by all the stories we shared. Silent tears stream forth, trying desperately to grasp what they have lost, each one a memory split in two—the other half held only by him. How much of him is in that box? How much of myself? And how can I ever open it again when every joy I placed inside is now a sorrow?

YEAR SEVENTEEN

"If neither foes nor loving friends can hurt you,
If all men count with you, but none too much;"

~Rudyard Kipling

Danzon in the Dandelions

I CRY MYSELF TO SLEEP and wade into dreams doused with his presence. I tell him I must let him go, that I have to keep on going, even though I don't know how. I know that across the cosmos he hears me, but all the same I wake weary, salt on my lips, seeing only sadness through my puffy lids.

Somehow, I will myself to pack my bags for our state's summer music conference. During my drive there, I replay all that has happened. Our world reels without him. State committees scramble to gather the work he was spearheading. His Big University Band frantically searches for a director, interim or otherwise. And all the while, my mind keeps returning to the list of concert programs he left lying on my desk. Surely he did not mean for me to do them. Surely he made some other plans with a more seasoned director. But as the days have unfolded, no other plans have.

I arrive at the conference, finding a suitable parking spot in our usual garage. Then, intending to stash my parking validation ticket until the journey home, I open a rarely used front seat compartment to find an emergency drum key I once tucked there.

A good director is never without one.

Next to it sits an old fortune I saved from one of our many meals out together. As I read its faded blue words, the voice I hear is his:

> "Some people never have anything
> except ideas. Go do it."

Next to my drum key, the sigil of Mr. F's mentorship, his wishes are alive around me, and I finally accept them. *"It is not broken beyond your means. Go do it."*

So I do.

I make a few calls, and when I return home I send an email application to the University bigwigs. I tell them I will conduct the year of programs he left with me, and in twenty-four hours I am sitting in their welcome meeting.

At the first rehearsal, the department chair conveys his condolences and introduces me to the band. It's clear to me many of them don't want to continue. They are thinking of quitting, like the students at our high school after his retirement. They want to play for no one else. I know the feeling. But I also know how to follow him now, and I will not make the same mistakes twice. I tell them my plans. No one questions them. No one quits.

I keep everything the same: section seating, rehearsal structures, concert schedules. I see there are ways I remind them of him, and I am not sorry for the way it makes us sad. We meet in the empty valley that should have been his and we play his songs, and we live the final lessons he left us.

The Danzon I've loved so dearly turns out to be highly anticipated by many students as well. One especially ardent percussionist, studying abroad from Mexico, pulls me aside one day after rehearsal to thank me for doing the piece. I can see its significance for him.

"It is a love song for my country," Lalo explains. "It evokes memories of my home and fills me with pride to hear it here, so far away from those who taught it to me."

Nostalgia. We all feel it: love for what we've lost, love for what we've left, beating its way into the world against our rough-hewn ribs. We let it grow in our rehearsals, and our first concert aches with it. Solo clarinet and claves fill the fan-shaped hall, and Mr. F is with us from our first breath.

I know the piece by heart and look only at my players, cradled by the wooden band shell at their backs. I feel the familiar conducting patterns my mentor taught me cross my body and some spiritual threshold, becoming a blessing over his band. Every eye is on me, including the brilliant blue ones of our new hire Eliza, who has joined our ranks in tribute to him. He is her teacher now too.

As the piece builds toward its best moment, lush with dulcet harmonies, an unexpected movement catches my eye from the back of the band. The percussion section steps side to side in union. *What are they doing?* I partially panic, my heart beating faster. Then, unexpectedly, all eight of them swirl and I realize...they are dancing.

Lalo has taught them his Danzon in secret, revealing it for the first time not in rehearsal, but under the heat of our stage lights, for all the audience and me to see. Unbeknownst to the rest of the band, their eyes beam brighter with every step, watching my reaction as their unexpected offering unfolds.

Often, concert band music impounds its percussionists behind endless bars of rest, sentencing them to count the beats filled by the rest of the band, but today they fill their tacet track with dance, elegant and tasteful and nostalgic. It's magic, and they know it; its meaning is too much, even for music. It's a gift no box could contain and one only they could give, shining from Mr. F's own section at the back of the band.

I will never hear the Danzon the same way. It will always be my favorite piece.

I spend the rest of the year driving from the Academy to the University—and eventually home, exhausted. I spend my Saturdays and Sundays sowing forget-me-nots in every empty inch of my garden and studying the notes Mr. F left in his scores. In every piece I find something sweet and share it with our university students. We discover in each program themes about love overcoming death. The percussion writing is insistent, and more than one piece ends with a solo flute carrying on when all the rest have ended.

His last program is called "Decades of John Williams." It's a program of Mr. F's crowd-pleasing, chop-busting favorites. It feels more like decades of Mr. F to me. Every piece has unquenchable spirit and hope. Each one says *keep going.*

Piece by piece, we heal ourselves with these breadcrumbs he left us. I write his name on every program and poster, leaving off my own and laying each one in my box at concert's end. We dedicate the entire year to him because, although his chapter may be over, his story certainly isn't. One lifetime is not long enough to complete the kind of work he was doing.

I wish I could have stayed there. Honoring his legacy. Performing his plans. It was always our deal. And I loved it so. I would have stayed longer, like kids after a concert, immune to all eventuality. But his hand was fading from mine in the darkness of that valley. I fumbled, reaching out for it, and my hand did find another, but it wasn't his.

One morning, when I sit with the first wisps of light, I find an email awaiting my reply:

Hi,

Sorry to send this so late, but it's been a difficult week. I have been stressed for most of this school year, especially the last few weeks. I was hoping at this point things might be easier and that I'd be in more of a groove, but it does not feel like that's happened yet. I'm having a hard time figuring out how much of this is normal to be feeling as a first-year teacher. I feel badly for causing you additional stress with everything else going on but any thoughts you have would be welcomed.

Thank you,

Eliza Lesperance

She stops me in my tracks: *"This is the next step, not just for her, but for you too."*

I've left my last assignment from him undone.

I read her words again, and I hear them as my own, coming back to me across time. I see my younger self in her and I know what she needs. So I let go of my mentor's hand—knowing he is with me in other ways—and turn to take hers.

His words, and now her words, encourage me onward. As much as I love the University, working both jobs has stretched me thin. I resign at the end of the year, his plans now complete, my search for myself now satisfied. I know if I continue to live the life he led, I will never have the time to tell our story, and it is one we all need to hear. I turn my attention to Eliza, and after years of writing letters of recommendation and notes to students who must inevitably leave, I write perhaps my most important letter yet.

Dear Eliza,

Thank you for your candor. I've been thinking, this week especially, that I wanted to tell you how proud of you I've been, but I was afraid to be too familiar. I wish I had told you sooner. I think most of the world doubts themselves. I often do. I can tell you if you keep going, it will get better, but not on its own. You must deliberately do the things you love, leaving their breadcrumbs in a box to revisit later, with the perspective only time can teach you. This job is hard. They all are. But you have not lost your opportunity, and it's never too late. I know you are learning the lessons you are supposed to.

These are normal first-year-teacher feelings. Honestly, they're normal human feelings: the hardship, the pain, the making-it-into-art that is to come. No matter what, move toward what calls you. Decisions made in love always work. Decisions made in dread always don't. I know. Each time you have a success, a concert, a festival, or just a simple moment, it will mean more for the days when you didn't. You will know the value of your work because of what it felt like when you started, what it asked of you every day, and where it led you in the end. And not to spoil it for you, but we are not at the end yet...

Since the beginning and always,

Lindsey

From then on, I spend my weekends writing stories for her, so she knows it is normal and she knows it is hard and she knows she can do it. Because I have no special talent, and I did. I start with sweet stories, but as time passes, I tell her sad ones too; there is value in all their broken pieces. I share my stories, not so she sees my successes, but so she won't wonder if it's worth it for as long as I did.

I teach her everything my teachers taught me: how to play each instrument and how to fix them, how to hold a baton and the band's attention, how to get started, how to keep going. I model what I believe is best practice in every interaction with her because I know the way I teach her is the way she will teach our students. Everything I want for them I must want for her too.

I realize our profession runs on these parallel tracks; if they are not aligned, we will get nowhere. We cannot help it. There is no detail we can afford to miss. I see her build her own box, strong and solid, from all the pieces around her, and I am not surprised to find little pieces of her in mine.

One Wednesday, when life is particularly difficult—when nothing goes her way, and people she is counting on let her down, and I know my words won't help—I take a chance.

"Hey," I say as the school day comes to a close, "do you want to go on an adventure?"

"Yes," she responds without any hesitation at all.

Courage, I think. *This one has courage. Or trust. Or maybe she figures it can't get any worse. Or maybe all of it.*

After the buses leave and we finish the work that would weigh us down, I run down the hall to the room that once was mine to find her. I lead her to a forgotten courtyard, where weeds grow wild within the walls of the school. Today it is filled with feathery dandelions. Their skeletons stand gray and translucent across every inch of the courtyard's crabgrass.

"Wish," I say, and she knows what I mean.

We hold the flowers for each other and set their seeds free with our breath. We dance our own Danzon through them and they fly in the air, and they stick to our feet, and they cling to our hair, and we laugh, and we wish, and we let our cares fly away, windblown. When not a seed remains on the stems at our feet, we watch them soar over the walls of our school's secret garden and out of sight.

"I liked that," she says, and even though the day was rough, she is smiling.

"Me too," I say.

We brush the seeds from our clothes, and I run back to my room. I take the clothespin from the corner of my computer, and when she isn't looking, I clip it to hers. She'll know what it means. She's read that story already. Then we take to the highway that hugs the river on our parallel drives home. She sticks right behind me the whole way.

In the reflection of my rearview mirror, I see her red car coming around the bend where the river creeps over the road when it floods. The sun is sinking low behind her, and the white-bark sycamores cast long shadows across the road we both travel. I've never seen them in this light because I've always been looking forward. She has shifted my perspective.

In the evening before bed, I undo my daily dress. I shed my teacher attire, and where my right arm meets my rolled-up sleeve, I find one last wish. I pluck it, and it clings to my forefinger, not as ready as the rest to be on its way. Is it meant for my box? I take it there, intending to add it. But I am a gardener, and I know a box is no place for a seed. It needs the sun to shine on it and the rain to water it, and it needs to seed others after it. And before all that, it needs my breath to set it wafting upon the wind. So I open my window, and I make one last wish, and I send it sailing out among the stars.

YEAR EIGHTEEN

"If you can fill the unforgiving minute
With sixty seconds' worth of distance run—"

~Rudyard Kipling

Time Will Do the Telling

"SEVEN A.M. IS THE PERFECT TIME FOR A ROCK BAND GIG!" I assure a flock of groggy-eyed aspiring teen rock stars as we unload our gear from the familiar box truck at the elementary school. They will their sleepy selves forward, too tired to talk, unconsciously falling in step behind me like a line of kindergarten ducklings. My smile is bittersweet, as Eliza and I both notice the imprint their elementary teachers made for only us to see.

I unlock the door to the towering new elementary school that stands on the footprint of our flooded first one. How much of our original school is still here? I reach out with every step to feel something familiar in the walls of this home I used to know. I feel our lost Atlantis, buried there beneath the mounds of flood mitigation systems, camouflaged with expertly designed landscaping. Our school still breathes loving endurance into everyone who ever knew her.

I turn back to my ducklings, who have long since abandoned their third-grade speed-walking skills.

They each hold the door for the next without being told to, and as they cross the threshold, I witness their unexpected transformations. Their eyes really open for the first time today as waves of memories splash them awake.

"Whoa! I remember the smell of this stairwell from reading group!" exclaims one singer, forgetting her fatigue.

"I've never even been in this school before," says another, who attended the other elementary school across town.

Chatter now fills the otherwise empty hallways as we make our way to their state-of-the-art theater. Atlantis is listening, and my students are finally awake.

The band members continue sharing stories of their favorite elementary days, as they piece together our drum set and sound system. Julian and a few other alumni, home from college, meet us there and join in setting up. Their hands work the practiced motions they've performed thousands of times with this group, and now others. Across the stage, cases click open once more.

"Here's the trick with the high hat," I hear one set player say to another newer member.

My heart aches at the absence of the one who taught me this very thing. Eliza looks at me while I watch them. She knows.

"We hide that piece inside the stand, so it isn't damaged when we travel."

My words—no, his—coming from the mouth of my student, passing this trade secret on to another, who will never know Mr. F's face and yet will know his mind.

Our engineer-dad-now-sound-guy, Mr. Wall, weaves with practiced stealth around the organized chaos of setup rituals. As one member, and then another is ready, we hear their musical signatures permeate the room. I know them as well as their voices. It is always the same fragments: long tones, leading to bits of scales and lip slurs, followed by articulated fanfares, announcing the warmup has begun. The singers gather around our piano player, who accompanies them through their favorite warmups while other instrumentalists quietly half-play along to see if they can truly play their scale patterns in every key.

The elementary school music teachers, Becky and Mr. Heart, sneak in from stage right to a torrent of hugs. The family reunion has begun. They ask if we need anything—since the flood, our district has worked to fill their shelves with every necessity—and we invite them to stay and play with us for the first song, which they do. While the teachers are getting their own instruments from their rooms, we go over a few things for today's field day performance. We are missing our twelfth graders since they are on their senior trip, so it's the first time our newest members sub into their positions. They are nervous and unsure, not knowing that this is the perfect first gig.

Our first set of the day for the intermediate grades is good, but tinged with the sharp self-awareness that inhibits an inspired performance. Our senior vocalists usually front the band, talking with the audience and announcing each new tune to give the other band members time to switch instruments. They know how to work the crowd, riff over transitions, and call everyone's attention to the instrumental solos throughout the show. Without them, awkward pauses arise and that electric energy we strive to create between the seats and the stage is missing. The songs are still fun, and the applause is still genuine, but when the intermediate grades leave for sack races and tug-of-war, we quickly huddle together like a football team before the primary grades descend upon us.

"The tempos were basically right, but the feel was draggy," offers our shrewd bassist.

"What happened getting out of the guitar solo, and into the

last verse?" asks a worried drummer.

They question and answer each other, unaware of the pitter-patter of tiny feet in the hallway.

"Okay, let's sub out 'Saturday in the Park' for 'Valerie' on this next one," I say.

"Can we start with 'Sweet Home Alabama'?" suggests a vocalist.

"Yeah, I think it is a better opener," the guitarist agrees.

"As long as we end with 'Shut Up and Dance,'" counters the drummer.

The deals are made, and just in time too. Our audience has arrived.

The band launches into "The Chicken" as the primary grades pour into the room, which already has a totally different vibe. The band now knows what they want, and this audience is immediately entranced. We announce the band members as they solo: new ones, seasoned ones, alumni, and finally, the elementary band director. All the solos are dynamic, and the crowd goes wild with surprise to see the hidden talent of their very own Mr. Heart finally on display. They all know he's a good one.

Legs swing from the seats as they sing along, regardless of whether they know the words. We needlessly encourage audience participation, and the room erupts in a rave of pandemonious dancing. The empty seats give way to mosh pits of flailing limbs, filling the aisles and flooding the front of the theater. Every single person is singing.

By the time we get to our closer we are not sure who is having more fun—the kids, the band, or the teachers. One thing is certain, however: There are no greater rock stars than these unseasoned underclassmen among a sea of five-, six-, and seven-year-olds. We are the first and best rock concert of their young lives.

As we finish, there is a surprise.

"We have an announcement! We have to sing 'Happy Birthday' to Mrs. Williams," my students say.

By the time the song is over, there is a small circle of birthday royalty at the front of the theater. We announce the names of all the crowned birthday kings and queens as elementary teachers scurry to the stage to get pictures with band members who once held their hands as line leaders. The teachers can't believe how their former students have grown, and the musicians glow at being remembered by name. Everyone has forgotten themselves in the joy of finding each other.

As the last of our kinder-crowd dances out the door and down the hallway to their next field day adventure, the band members trade solo after solo, playing for no one, and no reason, in an empty hall. Mr. Wall and Miss Lesperance smile, and so do I. We know "no reason" is the best reason and the most important audience member is the one you take with you everywhere.

The grounds crew has appeared at the door to help us load up, when a lone little one runs back to our stage as if approaching Taylor Swift herself.

"You are so beautiful, I think," says the kindergartener to our singers.

"Oh, thank you," the vocalists giggle in reply, both flattered by the sentiment and entertained by the syntax. Their biggest fan blushes and rushes back to her class. I know I will be seeing that one again.

Stories and laughter drown out the din of cases latching closed and drums being dismantled. Our assembly line gets everything back on the truck, and we are unloading again at the high school in no time at all. We congratulate each other and agree that we can't wait to do it again next week for our other elementary school.

When I return to my email inbox, there's a message from Mrs. Darling with a photo of our concert and a simple subject line: *Best part of our day.* It might be the best part of the week for some, or month for others, or maybe even longer, for teachers and students alike. It's a moment for our boxes. I know most of my students will find their professional successes in other fields and I am thinking, *Today might just be the best crowd they ever play for*, when a familiar train whistles outside my window.

I look up at the clock and smile. It's only 10:00 a.m.

Coda
The End

I IMAGINED MANY TIMES OVER THE YEARS what my floor would look like, flooded in rainbows of elementary artwork, photos, and letters. I told myself I didn't need to see them to know they were there, and that's true, but I also knew the contents of my box, and Mr. F's, called for something beyond its confines.

For a long time, I thought I would open my box when I retired, but when we danced in the dandelions I knew I would open it with Eliza. It was just one of the many ways we defied the trials of our days. I told myself I was sharing it for her benefit. But secretly I was still scared I'd see it wasn't worth it, and I couldn't face that alone. There had been so many sweet beginnings and endings I did not yet understand. I feared its pages would feel empty or obligatory, knowing the ones who wrote them were now off to other things, the Valley just a place they passed through.

On a September Saturday that feels like summer, Eliza and

I walk down the sidewalk from my house to the river. Acorns and oaks line the street of beautifully remodeled homes that no one could protect when the river broke its banks. Nature now invades this neighborhood, checkering its blocks with plots of crabgrass and clover where many flooded homes have since been demolished.

Our feet leave the pavement, and we step carefully over the chained entrance to the boat launch and down to the waterfront. It is quiet here, the still water muffling the busy freeway on the opposite bank. The river is low, and we wander past the silt line, where the water often flows. White river dust coats the leaves of wild forget-me-nots, but their petals are perfect, having bloomed in whites and pinks and blues since the river receded. No gardener's logic tends them out here.

Forget-me-nots are my favorite because they come back even though they are not really perennials. They do not set down roots and flower predictably in the same place from year to year. They reseed themselves, playing a coy game of peek-a-boo with their gardener each spring. You never know where you will find them. I've never seen them bloom in fall before.

Beside the boat path that widens into the river, we find the perfect place: a boulder jutting into the lazy current like a lighthouse. It is big enough for both of us and the contents of our boxes, so we sit, finding our place atop the layers of history that have been rounded by the river.

She shares hers first. There is a note of encouragement I wrote her on our first concert, a colored pencil portrait of her—baton in hand—sketched by a sixth grader, a few printed parent emails praising her concerts, and the notebook I gave her with a few penciled-in anecdotes she's found amusing. We smile and she makes me laugh with the stories she tells about each one.

"I've already opened it a few times," she says. "It helps."

I look down at mine.

"You don't have to share it if you don't want to," she assures me.

"No," I say. "It's okay. I want to."

"Are you sure?" she asks gently, as I pull the box from the tote at my side. She knows what it means to me.

"I'm sure. It's always better together," I say, brushing the years of dust from its lid.

She smiles. "You've really never opened this?"

"No," I say as I open it.

Inside, we view relics of the stories I've shared. Some still sting, just like I thought they would, but time has tamed the edges that would injure me. Most letters are old by now, happy little quips of thanks, most from students, some from colleagues and parents. We flip over the whole stack and start with the oldest ones, seeing the same story from the other side. The first one is folded in thirds and addressed like a real letter on the outside.

> From: Rose Winters
> Room: 17 (4th grade wing)
> To: Ms. Williams
> Room: Stage

Inside, it says:

> *10/18/11*
>
> *Dear Ms. Williams,*
>
> *I'm VERY excited to be in your band class. I have been looking forward to playing instruments for a long time. I did not know the flute was so heavy. It's bigger than it looks. I like the flute. I love being in band. Thank you for teaching me. Write back soon!!*
>
> *Sincerely,*
>
> *Rose*

We pick up another memory, from middle school.

12/20/16

Dear Mrs. Williams,

This year has made me appreciate music a lot and I know I'm not the only one. I've looked up to you all through middle school and I've decided I want to be a band teacher too. I hope you and your family have a Merry Christmas.

Best wishes,

Ashton

These time capsules inscribe each era of my post, like the layers of sediment that sit beneath us. I am surprised to find the notes that comfort me most are those that hold a bit of heartache themselves. Their sheets of loose leaf tell me that even though it's over, I made their difficult times here a little better.

May 5, 2018

So now that this year's NYSSMA festival adjudication is all over with, I'd just like to say thank you so much for helping coach me through this process. It really helped me LEVEL UP my playing! But seriously, all the early morning, short notice practicing made this difficult year so much easier. You always made it different and fun. So just thanks for all you did to help me.

Thomas

I can see that Eliza is moved by one letter in particular: Julian's. He didn't send it at the end of his senior year, when I expected it. He waited, the same way I waited to make my box. He sent it after a year of college, and when I first read it, I still felt like I'd failed him, that the pandemic had just derailed all we had accomplished. But when I read it with Eliza, it finally feels real, the way my being a band director wasn't real until Mr. F announced me at the conference.

On the first page, Julian thanks me and tells me what I taught him, but on the second he adds something else:

September 2022

Mrs. Williams,

Every once in a while, I question if what I am going to school for is what I really want to do with my life. Mrs. Williams—Thank You. You have shown me that I am following in the right footsteps. You changed my life. You gave me a true understanding and love of music. You've been my Dumbledor, my Gandalf, my guide. But even as I write these words, I think Harry Potter and Frodo would have been seriously lucky to know Mrs. Williams. So thank you for planting seeds that grow more for me each day and for nurturing them through it all.

Since the beginning and

Always your student,

Julian Finch

Somehow, I needed Eliza's outside eyes to see it for me, so I could know its significance. I'd spent so much of my time trying to make sense of these disjunct scenes, trying to arrange them in a path that led somewhere significant. But sitting here, I realize school doesn't always make sense. Our stories strain against all our best efforts to corral them, because they are not made for a path or even a box, and they widen whatever is forced upon them with every beat of their unruly wings.

"Live like it isn't going to hurt," I say to her.

I remember the desk drawer I opened on the first day in my flooded room. I remember the letters that were not mine and the fear that was and I am struck by what is not in my box: all that foolishness we usually focus on. From this perspective, Sisyphus's stone doesn't seem so much a struggle. I see what my teachers saw in me from what my students take from me. I find the teacher I've been seeking in myself. I just needed Eliza to help me see it.

I see the first letters I placed in my box, and my first assignment echoes in my ears:

And on the day you don't feel like being a teacher anymore, you need to open that box and read them.

Then I see the last letters, and feel my final assignment, still strong in my sails:

This is the next step, not just for her, but for you too.

Finally completed, these tasks are now linked. This learning, this letting go, has been my most important act of existence, and I see that even if we don't change the outcome, we change each other, and that matters.

"Fill your box and share it," I say.

I close the box, and she opens a book, and we sit with our boxes between us intending to read for a while by the river. As she reads aloud, I scan this familiar spot of mine for signs of life. Here I often see ducks, geese, and gulls, sometimes swans, and even herons, but today the river is empty and wide open. The sun warms the pages, matching the warmth of her words, and she is only three sentences in when I stop her.

"Look," I whisper, and she does.

I point to the edge of an island right in front of us. Down where the bank becomes the riverbed, a bald eagle has landed. If he sees us, he doesn't show it. He tucks his wings back and walks upon the broken bits of rocky riverbed until he reaches the water.

He dips in one yellow talon and then another. Then, as if testing the temperature and finding it to his liking, he bows his head and bathes like a sparrow in a birdbath. The water runs in rivulets down his back. He lounges there, toeing the current, not caring if his feathers function in the sky. Then he drinks deep draughts of the water that would weigh him down, and when he finally lifts his head, the river drips from his tawny beak.

After a while, he steps to the island's shore and suns himself on a rock much like ours. We watch him, half a river away, until eventually he takes flight and the remaining river droplets fall in all directions from his unfurled wings. He flies low for a long time, the tips of his wings sending ripples across water. Then suddenly he launches upward, as if diving into the sky, where he soars over forests of finches until we lose sight of him.

We sit together for a long time after he has left, feeling that the intersection of our paths isn't accidental at all. She reads and her words fill the air until the sun slants low over the pages. Then we tuck our boxes and our books in our bags, and led by both our teachers and our intuition, we wander by the river just a little longer.

The dark descends and the night sky widens before our eyes, leaving only air between us and the infinite. With seeds at our feet and stars overhead, we finally feel what once flooded us keeping us afloat. When at last we head for home, dandelions dot every inch of our path and we walk slowly with each other out Where the Valley Widens, drinking in its rapture, making wishes all the way.

ACKNOWLEDGEMENTS

My gratitude goes to my beloved family and friends who listened patiently to my chapters in their ragged beginnings. My appreciation goes to my brave editor, James Bock and to the Compass Rose Publishing Team, Bob Mrazek, Thomas Hurd, Diane Kane, and cover designer, Danielle Kane for believing in this little book and untrained author. My final thanks go with my teachers, and my students, and now with you reader, for walking Where the Valley Widens for just a little while.

AUTHOR BIO

Lindsey Williams has directed award-winning bands at all levels in the public schools since 2007. She graduated summa cum laude from the Boston Conservatory, earning her BM in flute performance, her MMED, and the Conservatory's Outstanding Music Educator Award.

She has directed Binghamton University's Wind Symphony and chaired numerous festivals and committees for the New York State School Music Association.

An active performer, conductor, and clinician, Lindsey lives with her family and cats in upstate New York. She still loves making music just as much as writing about it.

Connect with her at lindseywilliamsmusic.com.
Instagram: @LindseyWilliamsMusic
Facebook: facebook.com/LindseyWilliamsMusic/

www.ingramcontent.com/pod-product-compliance
Lightning Source LLC
Chambersburg PA
CBHW021221130626
46554CB00004B/1305